I Hate Selling

for the Fitness Professional

6 Steps to Making Serious Money
in the Fitness Industry

Ryan McKenzie
Allan Boress, CPA, CVA

Copyright © 2017 Training With Ryan.

All rights reserved. No part of this book may be reproduced, stored, or transmitted by any means—whether auditory, graphic, mechanical, or electronic—without written permission of both publisher and author, except in the case of brief excerpts used in critical articles and reviews. Unauthorized reproduction of any part of this work is illegal and is punishable by law.

ISBN: 978-1-4834-6269-1 (sc)
ISBN: 978-1-4834-6268-4 (e)

Because of the dynamic nature of the Internet, any web addresses or links contained in this book may have changed since publication and may no longer be valid. The views expressed in this work are solely those of the author and do not necessarily reflect the views of the publisher, and the publisher hereby disclaims any responsibility for them.

Lulu Publishing Services rev. date: 12/20/2016

Contents

About the Authors vii

Part 1 - Get Ready!

Chapter 1 - Something Had To Change 3

Chapter 2 - Who Is It All About? 9

Chapter 3 - Three Types of Trainers 17

Chapter 4 - Working Your System 27

Chapter 5 - Selling Redefined 38

Part 2 - Get Set!

Chapter 6 - Step 1 Do They Know That I Care? 45

Chapter 7 - Step 2 Ouch! Where's The Pain? 56

Chapter 8 - Step 3 Committed or Just Complaining? 65

Chapter 9 - Step 4 Top Dollar? 74

Chapter 10 - Step 5 Outside Influences? 84

Chapter 11 - Step 6 Real Results & Real Referrals! 93

Part 3 - Go!

Chapter 12 - Twelve Top Rainmaker Tips 105

About the Authors

Ryan McKenzie

Ryan McKenzie has worked in the fitness industry as a coach and personal trainer for over 12 years and has amassed more than 10,000 hours in 1-on-1, group, and team training. His knack for fitness and coaching runs deep – his father was a football coach, physical education instructor, and small business entrepreneur and his mother was a guidance counselor and educator. Through his initial struggles in sales in the fitness industry and lack of ability to reach those who needed help, McKenzie set out to change the way people thought about personal training and fitness professionals. Through his studies and daily applied work he has adapted the proven "I HATE Selling" Sales system into a practical and successful program that every fitness professional can use to grow their business and reach people the right way. He has since assisted individuals and teams grow their clientele, revenues, and profits, while increasing their quality of life.

McKenzie is an active member of the National Academy of Sports Medicine where is a Certified Personal Trainer and Performance Enhancement Specialist. He also holds certifications as a Parisi Speed & Strength Coach, TRX Suspension Training Instructor, as well as being certified in the Functional Movement System Level 1 & 2. McKenzie graduated from Rollins College with a degree in Psychology.

For more information: www.facebook.com/TrainingWithRyan

Allan Boress, CPA

Allan Boress is a CPA and veteran sales trainer with over 38 years of experience. He is nationally known as the sales training and business development expert for practices and service practitioners, having worked with more than 200,000 business professionals and 500 firms to teach the art of systematic selling, effective marketing, and client retention.

Boress is also the best-selling author of the original I Hate Selling training series of books, CDs, and workbooks. This is the ONLY training course in the world designed from scratch specifically to teach professional service providers how to interview, qualify, present, and close more sales opportunities.

As the way most new programs go, the I Hate Selling series was born out of necessity. As a newly minted CPA in 1979, Boress did not think he would have to get out there and SELL. In fact, it's part of the reason why he chose to be a CPA – don't people just show up at your door because they need you? Little did he know that what he did not learn in school was going to make or break his service business before it even started. He quickly discovered that he needed to learn how to sell and close contracts in order to survive. After months of reading sales books, listening to selling technique tapes, and attending frenzied sales seminars that didn't work for his personality, style, or industry, Boress decided to create his OWN sales and closing methodology for people just like him — people who hate selling. (Oddly enough people who hate selling are usually service providers such as accountants, lawyers, chiropractors, financial planners, dentists, graphic designers, freelance writers, engineers, architects, fitness professionals, and so on.) After interviewing more than 1,000 of the highest paid service providers in North America, Boress learned every aspect of building a professional practice including:

- Building a lifetime of powerful referral networks,
- Creating a personal marketing plan that attracts prospects and converts them to clients,
- And best of all, closing more sales for higher fees — faster!

Boress's accolades include:

- One of the top 16 Most Recommended Consultants in North America by Inside Public Accounting magazine.
- One of the 100 Most Important People in the Accounting Profession by Accounting Today magazine.

- The Instructor Excellence Award by ICPA Foundation for four consecutive years. This honor is only bestowed on the top five instructors out of over 200 candidates for excellence in client relationships and talent in audience interaction.
- Author of the Article of the Year, awarded for "The Three Biggest Mistakes Professionals Make in Marketing Financial Services" as published in The Planner.
- Best-selling author and creator of:
    - I Hate Selling Series books and audio
    - Professional Selling System book
    - I Hate Networking audio
    - Building Entrepreneurial People book
    - The 8 Biggest Mistakes CPAs Make in Selling audio
    - A Contrarian's Approach to Selling audio
    - The 3 Biggest Mistakes Entrepreneurs Make in Sales audio
    - Ten Rules of Effective Team Selling book
    - The Single Most Important Factor in Winning the Client audio

- Co-author and creator of:
    - 7 Hidden Secrets to Power Publicity for Small Business Owners audio
    - How to Create Your Life-Long Source of Never-Ending Referrals
    - Best Practices in Legal Marketing book
    - Best Practices in Personal Marketing For Professionals book and tapes
    - Best Practices in Building Your Personal Network for Professionals book
    - The Marketing & Sales Lessons from the 2004 Election resource

- Regularly published articles in:
    - The Practicing CPA

- o   The Attorney's Marketing Report
- o   The Practical Accountant

- Author of the lead stories, "Building Rainmakers" and "Stop Small Firm Drain" published in The Journal of Accountancy.

Boress is a Certified Public Account and Certified Fraud Examiner. For more information about Boress and his I HATE Selling program:

>   www.facebook.com/allan.boress
>   www.IHATESelling.com

Part 1 - Get Ready!

Chapter 1 - Something Had To Change

I Used To HATE Selling...

I still do, well, at least in the way most people think of selling. Maybe this is because I was really bad at sales, or maybe it is because of the way I was raised. I felt awkward when I would try to sell something even though I was normally a likable, easy going kind of guy. It just wasn't me, and it showed – especially in my paycheck.

In college I loved working out. If I wasn't on the baseball field practicing then I was in the weight room training. Immediately after graduation, I started an internship helping in a local weight room at a private school and then went on to get a job at the best athletic club in the area – which required that I SELL (and remember, I was really bad at sales). I also married my wife shortly after graduation, and very soon after that we were pregnant! So here I was, newly married, a baby on the way, and making little to no money. I started to re-evaluate my career. Sure I love what I do, but is it worth the financial uncertainty? Should I just get a desk job? Could this ever be a career where I can really provide the type of life I want for my family, or am I just doomed to barely get by for the rest of my life? When I realized that we couldn't pay our bills and we were falling deeper into debt, I had to face the hard reality of needing to move in with my in-laws six months after our honeymoon. It's in desperate times like those that you start to ask yourself those hard questions and doubt yourself. This was a tough but exciting time for our family.

I was told over and over again by leaders at my company, "You can't be in this for the money!" and "If you are here to make money, then you are in the wrong field, you are at the wrong gym!" So there I was feeling like I was drowning, wanting to find a way to make ends meet, wanting to find a way to get out of my in-laws house, if for nothing else but to prove to my new family that I can provide for them. You would've thought I had threatened their lives when I spoke up in a meeting and said, "Yeah, I get that but it can't be wrong to make a living too, right? We should be paid well for the service we provide." From that moment on I was branded as, "Ryan, the guy who only cares about money."

Now, don't for a moment think that I was this hopeless 24 year old kid with a young family to feed and no one would help me. That's not how it was. I had opportunity but I rarely took advantage of it early in my career. I was around some of the best trainers in the country and I let a lot of opportunities pass me by. You could say I was lazy, entitled, naive, inexperienced… whatever I was, I needed help and I didn't know how to ask for it.

Let's Take A Step Back...

I want to tell you a little about my life. If you're interested, read on and see if you can relate. This section is really where my beliefs were formed, and the rest of the book is how they were changed.

Growing up, my dad was a football coach and taught high school weight lifting; my mom was a high school guidance counselor. As you can imagine in a house of two teachers, we didn't talk about money much at all. Not that we were poor, but money and how to make it (i.e. sales) was not a regular topic of conversation sitting around the dinner table. My mom and dad were both incredibly hard workers. I remember thinking "How does my dad do it?" He would leave every morning before the sun came up and get to work before I ever even woke up. He would stay after school to coach, then come home and work on his own business – he ran recruiting tapes for high school football players. (College coaches were constantly in our house watching tapes, drinking beers, and talking football. It was pretty cool.) My mom wrote class curriculums for teachers in her spare time – she would work on personality training and counseling scenarios. She wrote continuing education courses for teachers. We weren't rolling in money, but we were comfortable and my brother and I never felt like we were lacking anything. But talks of sales? Being a salesman? How to build and grow a business? It was never brought up. It was almost a bad word, a negative thing that we didn't talk about.

Early in my life I fell in love with baseball. Man, I loved baseball. The only problem was, I couldn't hit. Not couldn't-hit-a-home-run, couldn't hit. But, was nicknamed the strikeout-king, couldn't hit. Still, for some reason I loved the game. I loved practice, I loved taking ground balls, I loved lifting, I loved conditioning, I loved the strategy. I loved all of it. I would lay around and think about it. I would have my dad hit me ground balls for hours. We even built a batting cage in our backyard. I thought and talked about the game constantly. But there was always someone better than me – a lot better than me. I was never on a team where I was the coach's first choice. But eventually something funny started to happen. All of my "all-star caliber" friends were quitting, giving up, and getting tired of the game. The kids that I was afraid to hit against and the kids that I was afraid would take my place on the team, just flat out stopped playing. The second it got harder, the second the coach yelled at them, benched them, said something negative to them, they were done. I guess those years of struggling and working hard instead of everything coming naturally to me (and having an old school football/weightlifting coach for a father) might have actually done something pretty good for me. You couldn't make me quit. I wouldn't give up. I would never give in, no matter how hard it got or how bad I was. No matter how they treated me or talked behind my back, no one was going to take this from me. I was going to play baseball.

I was cut the first time I tried out for my high school baseball team, and then I cried the whole way home. Apparently no one wants a middle infielder who is too slow, has a weak arm, and can't hit his way out of a wet paper bag. I remember telling Coach Wilkie "I'll be back in the spring."

That summer I worked harder than I ever had before in my entire life. I hit, lifted weights, threw thousands of baseballs, and then hit some more. From that point on, I decided that I would never let anyone work harder than me ever again. Sure, there were tons of kids who were better. But I wanted it more and I was determined to not only make the team but to start at second base, and I did just that.

After high school I found out that there still wasn't a lot of interest from colleges for a 5'7" 155 lb. kid who runs as fast as most 200 lb. kids and who struggles to hit the ball out of the infield. But I had decided that I wasn't done. I found a junior college in the panhandle of Florida (Madison

County, aka the middle of nowhere) and spent the year berated and belittled by a coach who took it personally every time someone so much as looked at him the wrong way. From there, I talked myself onto a wood bat summer league in Hendersonville, North Carolina at the base of the Blue Ridge Mountains. The coach liked my work ethic and grit and told me I had a spot on his team at another small two year junior college. It was there that I hit the highest batting average I had ever hit before in my life – .296! Yes, for all you non baseball fans out there, that means 29.6% of the time I stepped into the batter's box I got a hit – or 70.4% of the time I got out. I knew failure well. But I also learned how to win. As a team, we won 42 out of 61 games that year and we had played against some amazing talent – guys throwing 96 mph.

After two years I started to get a little home sick and wanted to come back to Central Florida, BUT I still wanted to play baseball. For my last two collegiate years I decided that I wanted to play at Rollins College in Winter Park, Florida, just down the road from where I grew up. The only problems were: they had never heard of Ryan McKenzie, they didn't need a shortstop, AND they didn't have any scholarship money left. So obviously I walked out onto the field at the end of one of their practices and introduced myself to the head coach. I asked if I could come for a tryout. He reluctantly agreed to let me come that weekend but made it clear that he was not very interested and by no means did he have any scholarship money to give me. I didn't care. I had already decided I was going to play there. I went to the tryout and played better than I had ever played before. I was given a place on the team and they even offered me a small scholarship. Turned out, the head coach used to be a hardworking, overachieving middle infielder as well, and I guess he had an extra scholarship lying around that he forgot to tell me about.

Rollins is where it all happened. No, I didn't make it big in baseball. I didn't get drafted or go to a semi-pro league like I had always thought I would. My athletic career of grinding it out and overachieving would end there. But something else happened at Rollins that changed my life forever... I met a girl.

Trying To Make Ends Meet…

Shortly after college, Grace and I married, and shortly after that we found out we were pregnant! I remember reading a card she gave me for my birthday that said "Happy Birthday to a great man, a great friend, a great husband and a great father!" I didn't think much of it at first, other than, she loves me, I have such a great wife, she even thinks I'll be a great dad one day. It was at this moment that she looked me in the eyes and said, "Ryan, I am pregnant. We are pregnant. We are having a baby!" We were so excited, I can't even describe the joy in my heart knowing that we were going to have a little one to hold and take care of. Even though he was unexpected he was never unwanted, we always knew we wanted to have kids. We just didn't realize that it would happen so soon! At this point I realized that we were very underprepared, we didn't know enough, we didn't have enough, we weren't disciplined enough and we needed to make a change. I knew that I needed to provide for my new and growing family, so I needed to do something that I had never done before. That meant going somewhere I had never been before. So, I went out and got a coach. Sound familiar? In baseball or any other sport when you're struggling, you go talk to your coach, ask for help, and get some constructive feedback. I started with my brother-in-law – an incredible CPA, CFO, and one of the most brilliant business minds I know. I also talked to one of my pastors who owns a branding company, leads and counsels people daily, and has a gift for marketing and reaching people in unique ways. These two men were my coaches. They would listen to me and give me advice. I would act on their advice and, guess what? Things started to slowly change. I went from spending my "downtime" at work and at home applying for other jobs and sulking, to actually building my business and refining what it is that I do, and more importantly why I do it.

Starting To Grow…

During this time, one of my business mentors, Peter Brunton, recommended Alan Boress' book I HATE Selling. I bought it. Read it. It made sense. I read it again. I highlighted key takeaways. I read it again. I took notes. Now, in between every training session I was nose deep in this book, reading, highlighting, learning about sales and become a businessman. It was that year that my business grew by 60% (my wife and I will be the first to tell you that 60% of nothing is still not very much). But the next year it grew by another 40% and the next year another 35% on top of that! This was not some get-rich-quick scheme, these were real results in real time. I was transforming the way I thought, I was getting practical help, and it was actually working! The third year of focusing and working hard on my sales and business skills I became the top revenue producing trainer in the country for my entire company. In the COUNTRY! I began to consistently bring in well over six figures in training revenue every year. If a kid, who only knew about baseball and working hard can grab hold of a book written for CPA's and learn how to sell, then just imagine what you can do when you sink your teeth into this same system!

This is why I wrote I HATE Selling for the Fitness Professional. I recommended the book to many of the personal trainers that I've worked with but it didn't stick because it was written for CPAs. So I asked the original author permission to re-write the book and the two of us worked on it together. This book is for people just like you and me, who love what we do but don't know how to push past the lid that is holding us back. For those in need of help, and, for the ones who are already killing it at the top and need a way to not burn out, this book is for you. How do you grow in this industry without completely draining yourself, or your family? It's not easy, but it is doable. I am doing it and it is helping me change people's lives. Decide right now that you will be one of them, and let's get to work.

Chapter 2 - Who Is It All About?

Something Has To Change…

There is a reason why sales books exist. It is the same reason why self-help books exist. Most people want to be a better version of themselves. And hopefully tucked within the pages of these small, promising books we will find the keys to unlock that person.

> That person I could be if everyone else could see how talented I truly am.
>
> The success I could have if the economy wasn't so bad.
>
> The quality trainer I could be if I worked at a better gym.
>
> The amazing schedule I could have if my boss would give me better hours.
>
> The amount of clients I could help if I had more referrals.

Just thinking about all of these "ifs" makes me start to feel anxious and uneasy. The persistent push for more without a reason other than "I want more" OR the constant fear of failure crippling every move we make cannot be the answer. There has to be another way. Something has to change.

This book aims to be a little different. It is not about selling, at least not in the way most people traditionally think about selling. I hate that kind of selling, and when you really think about it, deep down, you hate that kind of selling too. Just think about the word "sell" for a minute. What feelings come to mind when you imagine making the "sale," or worse losing the "sale?"

How do you feel when you know someone's trying to sell you something?

_____

How do you feel about convincing someone to buy something?

_____

When you think of a salesman what is the first thought that comes to your mind?

_____

The most common images are the pushy used-car salesman, the tiresome door-to-door salesman, or the grinding business-to-business salesman roaming their territory. I recently heard a story about how awful the water filtration salesman can be. It stuck in my head because of the utter disgust used to describe the story. The salesman came into their home and made them feel completely dirty and poor and flat out used manipulation to gain a sale. When I heard this story all I could think was, "Wow, I never want to be seen like that."

You likely have your own story of horrible salesmen and sales experiences. To be fair, there are great salesmen and saleswomen out there honestly working hard and helping people. But when you hear someone speak about "sales," what do you think? What do you feel? Where does your mind go? Are you really excited to make some money, or do you want to turn and run and crawl into your shell because it makes you feel so uncomfortable?

When it comes down to it, the reason this book is different, why it works so well, is that selling is not just about making money and it is not just about convincing someone to do something. True selling is simply helping someone find what is best for them and then offering it to them. Before we get into how to sell and the types of salesmen there are, we need to come to an agreement. Here it is – everything is sales. You might not like it, you might hate it, but it is true. You are constantly selling, all day, every day. Now if you have the wrong thoughts on what true selling is, that can be a completely overwhelming and scary thought OR it can be a tiresome, wearisome belief. If you believe "sell" is a dirty four letter word then you may have already put this book down. One of the major goals of this book, is to help you not only become a world class fitness professional, but also to have the correct belief about what selling really is.

Think about the last time you went out to eat with a friend to a restaurant that they had never been to before. "What should I get?" they might ask. You may reply, "Oh, you have to try the Chicken Marsala, it is the best I have ever had, you will love it!" or "I usually get the burger and fries, they are the best in town." Can you see it now? What were you doing there? You were selling. Look around. Think about it. It is everywhere. All day, people are selling and they don't even know it. When you get excited about something, when you believe in something, when you are passionate something, it is easy to talk about it, it is easy to sell, and you do it all the time.

The Right Attitude About Sales...

> The more you think about how bad you feel about selling, the worse you will be at it.
>
> The more you think about all you can gain from selling, the worse you will be at it.
>
> The more you make it about yourself, the worse it will be for you.
>
> The less you make it about serving others, the less service you will be able to provide.

This is hard to wrap your mind around but it is completely true. Take some time and think about that. If you can let that sink in and change you, it could change everything for you. That means that it is not about you at all, it's about them. They are your clients, your friends, your family, and everyone around you – every relationship that you have. This can either be incredibly freeing or incredibly terrifying. Are you willing to lose control to gain it? Are you willing to give up yourself and what is important to you in order to help others find what they truly need? Almost every trainer has an all about ME attitude. "How good can I be?" "What results can I give?" "What do they think about ME!?" And here is the beautiful part – the "all about ME" mentality doesn't end well for anyone, but almost everyone does it! This should immediately give you hope. Why is this beautiful? Why should this give you hope? Because by only changing one thing, I am immediately on my way to the top. Business is looking up, the economy is not so bad. Can you see how this changes everything? It's so simple that it's hard.

Throughout this book you will have the opportunity to actively participate in what you are reading and learning with self-reflection questions or challenges at the end of each chapter. Be honest with yourself while you complete them to the best of your ability. It is not enough to simply learn the information intellectually, you must put what you learn into action. You might find it helpful to put this book down during these sections, get alone and think about the questions by yourself. Or, get with a group of your peers and talk through the reasons you believe what you believe and do what you do. I do this with my team and people that I mentor weekly, monthly, quarterly, and yearly in different ways. It is important to know why you believe what you believe why you do the things you do. Remember, iron sharpens iron and if you don't have someone to sharpen yourself against, you will find yourself becoming quite dull.

Self-Reflection...

On a scale of 1-5 (1= no, never; 5 = yes, always) honestly rate yourself in the following statements. To help you dig deeper, when you read the questions, make notes and write down your thoughts. There are no right or wrong answers here. This exercise is simply to help you know yourself better.

I am ready and willing to change.

1   2   3   4   5

I love selling, it comes naturally to me.

1   2   3   4   5

I am very uncomfortable around people I don't know.

1   2   3   4   5

I think and care a lot about what others think of me.

1   2   3   4   5

I have a mentor and coach that I work with regularly and am accountable to.

1   2   3   4   5

Write It Down...

As you read the following summary statements and questions, take some time to write down your thoughts and answers. Again, answer honestly as this exercise is simply to help you know yourself better. You may notice the need to change the way you have been taught to think about certain areas in your life. You may also remember specific examples of why you feel the way you do about selling. Write these down and take some time to think about them. If you don't know who you are and what makes you, you, you'll have a hard time helping anyone else.

(1) It has been said that change is never easy and no one likes change but those who desire to do great things seek out change in their lives BEFORE it gets to a point where they have to change. Do you already see areas in your approach to selling that need to change?

_____

_____

(2) Everyone has their own thoughts and feeling about selling. Some claim to love it, others fear it, and many hate it. But the fact remains that few do it well. Do not worry about having the correct thoughts about sales right now. Instead notice, maybe for the first time, what your feelings are towards selling. Your ability to control your emotions will dictate your success more than you can imagine. Now is the time to take account of how selling truly makes you feel.

_____

_____

_____

_____

(3) Can you walk into a room and become friends with the first person you see, or are you more reserved, taking time to survey the room? There is no one personality type that makes you more or less successful in sales. You don't need to change everything about you, BUT it is vital to know how you are wired. What is your go-to reaction when put in front of new people?

_____

_____

_____

_____

(4) Do the thoughts of others consume your mind? Do you find yourself arguing or competing with others in your head when they haven't said anything at all? This insecurity will undermine your success more than

almost anything else. This will be the cause of defeat for many, and it will drive others to seemingly rise to the top. Whether you are at the top or the bottom, constantly striving to outdo and prove everyone around you wrong will eventually leave you crushed on the inside no matter how good everyone on the outside thinks you look.

_____

_____

_____

_____

(5) You can grind, you can hustle, you can go all-in, but until you have a mentor guiding you and helping you, you will always feel alone. We weren't made to go at it alone. Your clients won't see real results until they get real with you and make it personal. Neither will you. What do you need in a mentor?

_____

_____

_____

_____

Put In The Work...

After you have taken some time to reflect go and watch Simon Sinek's TED Talk called, 'How Great Leaders Inspire Action.'

https://www.ted.com/talks/simon_sinek_how_great_leaders_inspire_action

What do you think your "WHY" is right now after watching this short talk?

_____

_____

_____

_____

_____

_____

_____

_____

For The Bold…

Let me know your "why." Viktor Frankl says in Man's Search for Meaning that "Those who have a 'why' to live, can bear with almost any 'how'." Share yours with me and the rest of the world and inspire someone today: www.facebook.com/TrainingWithRyan

Chapter 3 - Three Types of Trainers

Which One Are You?

When it comes down to it there are three types of trainers in the fitness world. No, I am not simply talking about weight loss, body building, sports performance or some other type of specialist. I am also not talking about extroverts or introverts or other personality types. Knowing your niche, your programming, your clients, your personality and where you are best suited to help them is extremely valuable and something I coach my team to be aware of on an almost daily basis. But for now I am talking about something different altogether. This is about what you truly believe about yourself and about others. You could have any type of certification in any field with any client base and with any personality and you can choose to be one of these types of trainers:

> The Faker
>
> The Taker
>
> The Rainmaker

Without going any further, I realize that we all want to believe we are the Rainmakers. We want to say that we feel sorry for the Fakers and hate the Takers. We want to be the Rainmaker, the one who makes it happen, brings in the money, helps the most people, has the most successful clients, is known as the one who has all the answers. But are you? How do you know? How can you be sure?

The worst thing would be to be standing in the shoes of a Faker or a Taker and to not even know it. So my goal here is simple: I want to step on your toes just enough to get you to move your feet. Once you know, then you can do something about it. Once you start to do something about it, then you can start to become good at it. And once you become good at it, then you can start to really put some time in to perfecting your craft.

Let's take a quick look at the Faker, the Taker, and the Rainmaker and see if anything resonates within you. I know, personally, even as I am writing this, I am still finding the Faker and the Taker buried deep inside of me on a daily basis. The more I ignore it, the more it grows. But when I can honestly say, "Yes, that is me, and I don't like it!" that is when I can start to do something to change it. So be honest with yourself and dig in, it's the only way to grow.

I Am A Faker
Common Phrases Heard From Fakers:

> "It's not my job to sell people, it's my job to train people."

> "I give good workouts and that should sell itself."

> "It's not about the money. I am not in this for the money."

> "I wish they would just leave me alone and let me train. That's why I am here."

> "I can't stand how they train, they aren't helping anyone."

> "The economy is really bad right now."

> "It's just a slow day in the gym I guess."

> "If they want it they will ask for it anyway."

> "I don't want to come across as too pushy."

> "Let me know if you need any help."

> "I'm not the salesman type."

6 Excuses I Make All The Time When The Faker In Me Fakes

1. **I'm too busy.** I don't have time to sell myself, my life is crazy busy. I am recently married, my newborn is at home, my parents, my in-laws, my friends, my own workouts, my problems, (you can insert your own life here). I just need my down time...

2. **I don't like it.** In fact, I hate selling. I hate that feeling I get when I try to sell to someone. I feel awkward, uncomfortable, and unsure of myself.

3. **I don't know how.** If I knew how, then I might be able to, but no one ever taught me. As it is now, every conversation and orientation ends with a strange pause where I am holding a contract for training sessions in my hand, saying some combination of "Well if you... we could... No? That's ok... let me know if you need anything..."

4. **I hate to fail.** Every time someone doesn't buy sessions I feel like a failure. I am letting down my family, my boss, myself. It means I'm not good enough or I don't know enough. I shouldn't be in this job. I'm not even a salesman, I am a trainer. They should just hire salesmen to sell the training for me.

5. **I'm not paid to.** What does it matter? It's just an extra session that I don't get paid that much for anyway. And it's not like I get a bonus or anything, at least not a good one. After all, I'm doing better than my buddy over there, so I am fine where I am. I just like to focus on training and being a good trainer, not seeing more people. I don't want to be greedy. Besides, I am doing fine right now.

6. **I hate it here.** Everything here is always changing. My goal changes every year, or I don't have any goals. There is no one to lead me, or there are too many people telling me what to do. Nobody understands me and nobody cares, or everybody is a critic.

Let's go back to our belief for a moment. Where are my eyes focused when I am the Faker? It's all about ME, MYSELF, and I. And the worst part is, something comes up every day to get me to look back at myself and make another excuse about why I can't/ won't/ shouldn't/ didn't/ make it.

It's always, "My boss is..." "The economy is..." "My location is..." "The weather is..." "My clients are..." The excuses go on and on forever unless you put them in check.

So the obvious advice is "STOP MAKING EXCUSES!" But is it that simple?

I really was the Faker when I started in this field right out of college. I was barely in the building a month and I was making excuses about why everyone else had more clients than I did. Once I realized it, I knew it had to change. So I went at it as hard I could.

Maybe, you are seeing yourself here too. It's a tough place to be and it's hard to change, but it can be done. When you realize it, it starts to bother you and it should. It just doesn't sit right and you know something has to change. So what do you do? Jump right in? "No more excuses! I need to sell and sell fast! I'm going to pick up the slack and make some serious money here!"

But hold on for a second, the pendulum swings the other way as well. If you don't go about this change the right way, you will quickly become the Taker. It happens faster than you can imagine.

I Am A Taker
Common Phrases Heard From Takers:

> "I'll do whatever it takes to succeed."

> "I need to make more money."

> "I'm going to train everyone."

> "You shouldn't train with them, you should train with me."

"First time is on me."

"I just want to train, all this other stuff gets in my way."

"If this place would do a better job at... I'd be where I want to be."

"If you sign up now, then I'll..."

"Let's make this happen, no more excuses. What's it going to take to get you going today?"

6 Mistakes I Make All The Time When The Taker In Me Takes

1. **I grow too fast.** I'm not making the money I want so I'll do whatever it takes to grow my book of clients and my paycheck. I push to the point of getting the reputation of being a used car salesman and always trying to sell something else. Large group training and more members makes me more money so I do anything I can to grow the numbers.

2. **I talk too much.** If they just knew what I knew, then they would definitely buy from me. It's up to me to tell them everything there is to know about physical fitness in order to convince them. They need to know exactly what we are going to do, how we are going to do it, when we are going to do it, and they need to know it all right now.

3. **I don't know when the sale is made.** I talk to a lot of people that are ready to start training and sign up for memberships about half way through the conversation. But for some reason, by the end of our talk they need to go "think about things," and they don't always come back. It's almost like I should have stopped talking half way through and had them sign up when they seemed ready.

4. **I assume answers instead of asking questions.** Whenever I see a new member walk into the gym I am really great at knowing exactly what he or she needs right away. It's a gift. I can tell what

they are thinking and feeling, and since I am such a great trainer I can tell exactly which exercise program and classes to put them in right away. If they don't buy it then they were probably too lazy to be here anyway.

5. **I beg for business and end up giving it away.** I'm always getting people to come try my new group or program. I can usually convince them because the first one is on me! This is my go to when I am trying to gain a new member or a new client – give it away for free, get them hooked, and they'll come back. It's what I've always done. It's a numbers game really. If I just throw them in, they may stick and come back. But if not, then it's on to the next one.

6. **I am in this all for myself.** This is my business and it doesn't matter what anyone else is doing. I run my training, gym, sessions, classes, the way I want to. Nobody can tell me what to do. Who better than me to help my clients? Sure, I learn from the superstar trainers online and I have some certifications, but why would I want to share with or learn anything from my competition? I don't want them stealing my secrets.

Takers usually don't make excuses, at least not as much as Fakers might. They seem to be confident and hardworking most of the time. They are at least trying, but if they aren't careful they'll make some HUGE mistakes.

The obvious advice here is "SLOW DOWN, DON'T MAKE MISTAKES!!!" But that doesn't always work either.

At this point you can likely see the tendency to be a Faker or a Taker, or a little bit of both. And to be quite honest, I have personally made all of these excuses and mistakes myself. They are thoughts I have had and beliefs I have seen in the trainers I have worked with as well. They slip in so quietly, you don't even realize that you are becoming the Faker or the Taker until it is too late. It is almost like a disease below the surface that you don't realize is there, eating away at your beliefs and destroying your attitude. Before you know it, you don't even remember why you got into this "job" in the first place.

Fakers make excuses, Takers make mistakes. We will get into what makes a Rainmaker later, but for now – who are you?

Self-Reflection...

On a scale of 1-5 (1= no, never; 5 = yes, always) honestly rate yourself in the following statements. To help you dig deeper, when you read the questions, make notes and write down your thoughts. There are no right or wrong answers here. This exercise is simply to help you know yourself better.

When something goes wrong, my first reaction is to cover it up.

1   2   3   4   5

When I am on top of my game, I want everyone to know.

1   2   3   4   5

It's not usually my fault when things don't go right.

1   2   3   4   5

I almost exclusively think about myself and the benefit that I will get when selling.

1   2   3   4   5

I often think about my client and how they can benefit when I am selling.

1   2   3   4   5

Write It Down...

As you read the following questions, take some time to write down your answers. Again, answer honestly as this exercise is simply to help you know yourself better. As you take time to reflect, you may see the Faker and the Taker emerge in your thinking. Don't shy away from them. Search them out, leave nothing uncovered. Be as honest as possible. Write down the areas where you see yourself becoming the Taker and the Faker and think about why you lean that way in those situations.

(1) Nobody likes to look bad. But how do you respond when it goes poorly and it is your fault? Do you shift the blame? Cover it up? Pretend like it will all be alright? Does the way you react here sound more like The Faker or The Taker? What about your gut reaction needs to change?

_____

_____

_____

_____

(2) Everyone likes to look good. But how do you respond when everything goes perfect? Do you gloat? Take all the praise? Act like you're a big deal? Does the way you react here sound more like the Faker, the Taker, or the Rainmaker? What about your gut reaction needs to change?

_____

_____

_____

_____

(3) If you think you did nothing wrong at all, odds are, you did. What does the way you respond in times of trouble say about who you tend to be in relation to The Faker and The Taker?

_____

_____

_____

_____

(4) You know the feeling you get on those days when you nothing can go wrong? Those times you are on top of the world? What does the way you respond when things are going great say about who you tend to be in relation to The Faker and The Taker? Why?

_____

_____

_____

_____

(5) No-one wants to be the Faker or the Taker, but take a realistic look at what is actually going through your mind when you are working with someone. Which way do you tend to lean the most and why? Most likely you're a bit of both at different times, but recognizing the Faker and the Taker within you is the first step to removing them.

_____

_____

_____

_____

Put In The Work...

Take some time to reflect on how you can sometimes be the Faker and the Taker, but don't stop here. Go to the five closest people to you in your life. Those who will be brutally honest with you. Explain the idea of the Faker and the Taker to them and ask them if they see any of those characteristics in you. After they've answered, ask them again and give them permission to be even more brutally honest with you because you want to grow. (We all know they were just a little too nice to you the first time around!) Then come back here and write down what they see. How does this line up with how you feel and what you see yourself?

_____

_____

_____

_____

_____

_____

_____

_____

_____

For The Bold...

I'd love to hear your lists. Be open and honest about who you have been and who you want to become! Make a 1 minute video summarizing these thoughts and post them at www.facebook.com/TrainingWithRyan.

Chapter 4 - Working Your System

It's Time To Regain Control...

The top Rainmakers, no matter the field, all stick to a system. Without a system you are doomed to failure. Most fitness professionals know that they should have a system but they hate the idea of actually following through and using this system. It is too confining, limiting, structured, or unoriginal for what they want to do on a day to day basis. But Rainmakers follow their system and they follow it well. The Fakers and the Takers are too worried about what everyone thinks about them to change what really matters. If you remember back to what the Faker and the Taker usually believe, it can quickly turn into an "all about me" attitude. "It's my workout." "It's my program." "It's my group." And the idea of a system feels like you are taking all of the control away. It feels as if all of the freedom and creativity is being eliminated. But, it's actually quite the opposite.

Step out of the realm of fitness and think about this. Tell a comedian to "be funny" and nothing comes out. Tell an artist to "create something" and they've got nothing. Tell a writer to "write" and all of a sudden writers block hits hard. But, ask the comedian what he thinks about a certain topic, give the artist a median, give the writer a topic that he cares about and all of a sudden their true brilliance comes to life. Give them direction, and freedom and creativity are maximized. Remove all structure and they are forced to recreate the wheel every time they get to work. Rainmakers in the fitness industry are no different. They realize that true creativity and control are peaked within the right system. The most successful fitness professionals do not choose exercises for their clients based on how new or trendy the workout is. They use and follow the best system for each specific clients. The same holds true when selling. Rainmakers are constantly working on themselves, developing the right attitude in order to provide an incredible experience for their clients. If we have the wrong attitude, if we come at this with a "me first" approach, the system won't matter, nothing will work – at least not for long.

Most of us hate the idea of being sold to. We don't want to be bothered or badgered. However, we also get annoyed when we are looking for something and we can't find someone to help us. How did you feel the last time you walked into a store, needed help finding a solution to a specific problem, and you couldn't get anyone's attention? It was frustrating right? This is just as exasperating a sales experience as being badgered. Neither the Faker nor the Taker are there to help you discover what you need. And that is the key to successful selling – discovery. Selling is not telling. Your job as a fitness professional is not to tell people what they want, but rather to help them discover their needs and offer a solution, all within the best experience possible.

This is why we must redefine selling. We must change our attitude toward sales, and we must do it now.

So, is selling good or bad? Right or wrong? Rabbi Daniel Lapin, author of Thou Shalt Prosper, says that sales is one of the most noble ventures. When you truly serve other people and help them obtain what it is they really want, you make sales. Every dollar that you receive for your work is a certificate of appreciation!

3 Attitude Shifts Crucial for Success...

1. **It's Not About Me, It's About Them.** Remember, it's all about the clients' experience. Not your bottom line, not your reputation, not your experience. From the moment they walk in the door, or even from the moment the phone rings, make it about them and they will be all about you. Think about it this way. Why is Disney World at capacity nearly every day? Why do people pay premium prices to endure long lines for short rides in the hot sun? The answer is simple – it's the experience. Disney has mastered the art of creating magical experiences and providing you with exactly it is you didn't know that you really needed. Not just fun

with your family, or fun with your kids, but actually to feel the freedom to be a kid again yourself!

You may be a great trainer and know exactly what your clients need to see results but sadly, results are not enough. They will always pay more and come back more consistently for the best experience. It's up to you to provide them that experience. And if you cannot, they will be gone.

All of the information anyone ever needs to get in shape is already on YouTube, Facebook, blogs, DVDs, apps, etc. Anyone can earn a certification, buy a book, or sit in on a conference, and probably for much less than they would pay you in the long run! So why on earth would anyone come to you for advice or training? Why should they pay you? The answer again is simple – the experience you provide for them. You must be able to create a tailored program to help them reach their goals, all the while encouraging their progress and celebrating their milestones.

Remember: the Fakers don't even realize they are supposed to be creating an experience. The Takers think they are the focus of the experience. But, the Rainmakers know that it is all about their client's experience.

2. **There Is No Such Thing As A "Slow Day."** How many times do you see trainers teach classes or run large groups and have 20, 30, 50 people show up? Of course, the trainer feels great because they made more money, but mainly because "so many came to see me." And they should feel appreciated. Without their class the participants may otherwise be at home watching someone else's workout with horrible form, doing the same workout every day, or not doing anything at all. The trainer is the one responsible for creating the atmosphere, the excitement, and the excellent workout. And people come because the trainer is good and because they want to believe that they can be too.

But what happens on those days when they don't come? Let's say you normally have a decent size group or class and one day attendance is down. Or you normally have a decent schedule, filled with one-on-one clients, and small groups and people start skipping out for the day, week, month. What if all of your new member appointments don't show up or don't follow up like you expected? Do you chalk it up to "just a slow day at the gym," "bad weather," "people are lazy"? Most trainers do. Very few will take the time to deal with those nagging, uncomfortable thoughts that are deep in the back of their mind. You know you've felt the nagging, and these thoughts are likely familiar to you: ... The best in the world deal with these thoughts all the time. But instead of ignoring them or running from them, they deal with them. And that's what makes them the best.

Now, I am not saying that we need to sit around and sulk and stay stuck in these thoughts. But, we cannot live in denial either. And unfortunately, most of us live here – where everything good that happens is because of us and everything bad that happens is because of someone or something else. We must step back into reality and take a good look at what we do that contributes to great days and what contributes to poor days. I realize that this is so hard to do, not because it is actually difficult or complicated but because it is very uncomfortable and frightening. Deep down we are afraid the answers could very well be "I'm not good enough." "They really don't like me." "I don't even know how to get better." "I'll never be as good as…"

It is good to have scheduled time each week to allow yourself to sort through these thoughts and questions, and to think and dream. "Where am I Faking right now?" "Where am I Taking?" "What do I need to improve?" Write down your thoughts and solutions and then actually do something about it. If you want to take ownership about the great job you did when you brought 50 people into a class, you need to make sure that you are also taking ownership when no one showed up. And yes, sometimes those days happen, and they are not fun.

Take responsibility for what happens on your watch, with yourself and with your clients. If they can't lose weight because they eat too much outside of the gym, guess what? You haven't motivated them enough and you haven't given them enough accountability. If they can't afford the training, guess what? You haven't showed them enough value and you don't know them well enough to be able to solve their problems. If the drive is too far or the hours are too tough or they are too busy, guess what? You have failed to show them how valuable you are and how worth it you are. We must have this attitude, we must not settle for placing the blame on others. If you bear the burden of responsibility now, you will be able reap the rewards of making it rain later.

Remember: the Fakers chalk it all up to luck and outside circumstances. The Takers take all the credit when it goes well. But, the Rainmakers regularly make time to take a good hard look at themselves and how they can get better. It sounds so simple, but it is rarely done. This is why they are consistently the best.

3. **Using A System Frees Up Creativity.** Chances are, you are creative (even if you don't see yourself as the creative type). You design workouts and programs for people and are constantly molding and shaping their future lifestyle with every piece of advice you give.

   When you hear, "follow the system," the thought that screams out from our creative minds is, "No! I don't want be like everyone else! You can't make me! I'm good because I am creative and you want to take that creativity away from me?!"

   I know this because I've felt it too. And no, I am not telling you to sell out or give up your creative brain and just become a cookie cutter robot trainer that copies and pastes workouts from a magazine from one client to the next.

   I'm talking about freeing your mind, allowing creativity to truly thrive, and getting rid of the burden of reinventing the wheel every day, every hour, every client. A good system can transform a good trainer with a limited book of business to a great trainer with a practically unlimited opportunity for growing your business and for making a difference in the lives of more people around you.

I had a trainer that worked for me who was insanely talented. He understood people, could sell, progressed his clients well, and got them great results. He could seamlessly move between textbook training and getting creative with new exercise. I never once had to say anything to him about how he worked with his clients. But here was his downfall, and most likely many of yours as well: he felt too busy. He had trouble taking new clients because he felt like he was underwater already (he was not, not even close). But our perception can be our reality and it is hard to change that. What was his real problem? He didn't follow a system. He was naturally good and instead of planting those natural abilities into a good system and watching them grow and produce an amazing crop, he was growing slowly. Gaining a couple of clients, losing a couple of clients. But all the while feeling like he either can't handle what he has or that he doesn't have enough!

We have all felt the pressure of being under someone's thumb and hearing "It's my way or the highway." As trainers, we love the freedom of being out from underneath that proverbial thumb. The freedom to grow a business the way I want and to work when I want is amazing. But if you are not careful, that freedom either becomes a cruel task master that won't let you take a day off for yourself OR won't pay you well because you take too much time off for yourself (neither are fun, I've been in both scenarios). This is exactly why we need proven systems implemented into our training and sales processes. A good system recognizes the greatness within you and allows it to flourish. It shows you when to push and when to rest.

Imagine if you didn't have that overwhelming, nagging anxiety when it came time to close a deal. Imagine if you didn't have to call random people to see if they might want to join your gym or your group. Imagine if you didn't have to come across like a slimy salesman when you walked through the gym. What if you actually saw real-life referrals start to come your way? What if you were so good at selling, it didn't even seem like you were selling but serving? This is what I HATE Selling is all about.

Comfort or Change?

We change by breaking out of our comfort zone everyday. By looking and searching for those things that make us uncomfortable and then grabbing them head on and tackling them to the ground until they become second nature. How can you expect to inspire someone to show up day in and day out and be put through a grueling workout (which very well may be easy for you) if you aren't also willing to go through grueling changes in areas in your life. You must lead the way and yes, it begins with your attitude toward change. If you won't change, you'll begin to notice that the people drawn to you are those who won't choose to change either. You will reproduce yourself in those that follow you. Remember that.

The Faker hears about using systems and says one of two things:

> "I don't know… that seems like a lot of work."

> OR

> "I don't know… I think I'm alright doing what I'm doing. We'll just see what happens."

The Taker hears about using a system and says one of two things:

> "I don't need anything, I'm great."

> OR

> "I am going to make so much money off these people!"

The Rainmaker hears these three points and immediately looks at themselves in the mirror and asks:

> "Is that me? Where can I sharpen up? Where can I be more efficient and help people more?"

Self-Reflection...

On a scale of 1-5 (1= no, never; 5 = yes, always) honestly rate yourself in the following statements. To help you dig deeper, when you read the questions, make notes and write down your thoughts. There are no right or wrong answers here. This exercise is simply to help you know yourself better.

I have a focused, systematic approach to training.

1   2   3   4   5

I have a focused, systematic approach to sales.

1   2   3   4   5

I have a focused, systematic approach to service.

1   2   3   4   5

I love change.

1   2   3   4   5

I find myself embracing change and following through with it often.

1   2   3   4   5

Write It Down...

As you read the following questions, take some time to write down your answers. Again, answer honestly as this exercise is simply to help you know yourself better. You may see areas where your attitude does not line up with other Rainmakers. Many people have different systems, theories and approaches but attitude is something that spans all fields. With the wrong attitude, it won't matter how great of a system you have. But with the right attitude and the right system, the sky is the limit.

(1) I know a system sounds boring to those of us that lean more toward the creative side. But you cannot just shoot from the hip and expect to hit the target every time. What is your approach? What about it needs to change?

_____

_____

_____

_____

(2) Think about what you do when you are with a potential client. Is it the same every time? Does it change often? How do you feel when you are trying to close the deal and get them started?

_____

_____

_____

_____

(3) We often only focus on sales and training but without world-class customer service these two can't hold up on their own. Do you have a proactive service plan? Are you always playing fireman, running around putting out fires?

_____

_____

_____

_____

(4) How do you really feel about change? Don't gloss over this. What is your gut reaction? Be genuine, be honest. If you find yourself hating change, ask "Why?"

_____

_____

_____

_____

(5) In which areas have you allowed yourself to become too comfortable? How do you plan on changing this desire for comfort instead of a desire for change?

_____

_____

_____

_____

Put In The Work...

Why should someone pay their hard earned money to train with you, when they could train with someone else down the street, read an article, watch a quick video, or even get certified themselves? Take some time and think about this. The answer has to be more than "I care" or "I'm the best."

Can you think of 10 real reasons that someone should train with you?

Go deeper here – what truly sets you apart from everyone else?

10 Reasons Someone Should Train With Me

1. _____
2. _____
3. _____
4. _____
5. _____
6. _____
7. _____
8. _____
9. _____
10. _____

For The Bold...

Go back to your list of 10 reasons that someone should train with you and narrow it down to your top three real reasons. Refine them and then video yourself saying them. Be genuine, be excited, and be real. Now watch your video. Do you believe yourself? What do you think a brand new client is thinking? Would they believe you? If the answer is no, get back to work, then send your videos to me for feedback: www.facebook.com/TrainingWithRyan

Chapter 5 - Selling Redefined

Who Is The Best Salesman You Know?

When I ask, "Who is the best salesman you know?" I am not talking about the salesiest, the pushiest, or the loudest salesman. Not the "What can I do to get you in this car today?" or the "Man do I have a deal for you!" salesman. If any of these examples are still what you envision, I challenge you to think about sales in a new way from this point forward. I understand that it can be extremely difficult to make this shift in your mind especially when so many of us have such an aversion to the word "sales."

We need to redefine selling using the attributes talked about in the beginnings of this book. A good salesman is someone who genuinely shows that they care for the best interest of the person they are working with, someone who wants others success even more than their own, and someone who creatively works within a system. A Rainmaker does not just make sales, or take someone's order, a Rainmaker inspires action.

Using this newly defined idea of sales, I'll ask you again

"Who is the best salesman you know? Why?"

Hopefully your eyes are opening up to great salesmen all around you that you never thought of as salesmen. Here is one that not many think of – your doctor.

I know what most of you are thinking "Huh? Doctor's don't sell anything." Some trainers have it out for doctors because some of them often prescribe pills and medication instead of a healthier lifestyle, but let's focus on good doctors that provide a more holistic approach instead of handing out prescription after prescription for more and more pills, pills that you need to take pills to cure the side effects of other pills... (You get the idea).

Think about what happens when most people go to an excellent doctor. You walk in and talk to him, you tell him all about your concerns and your pain. He listens and asks some great questions, and then listens some more. When it is all said and done, he has diagnosed the problem, gives you his professional opinion and tells you exactly what to do. If you are smart, you go and do exactly what he said to do. Rarely do people question their doctor when he says "take this pill," "go see this specialist," "take some time off." It is often almost blind obedience. Sure, we might have questions and personal trainers being in the health and fitness industry question traditional medicine more than most on some level. But, is this really a good example of sales? Sure it is! Think about what happens when you go to see a doctor. This man or woman that you barely know convinces you to do things or buy things and you do it. Why? How? Because he has a white coat? Because he has been in school for so long? Because he has a plaque on the wall or his name on the door? The real reason is simple – the very best doctors speak from a level of expertise that others around them just don't have. They bring their knowledge in a very caring, but also professional attitude. He has what will make us better and he wants us to get better, but if we don't do what he says then he can't help us and he knows it. We never feel like he is selling us anything, but he is the whole time! And honestly most doctors probably don't even see it as selling and that's the brilliant part!

True Rainmakers have learned to become like doctors. No, not in that they practice medicine or put up plaques and diplomas on their walls or wear white coats. They use the same systematic approach when selling that the best doctors do every time they see a new patient: they find their client's pain and offer a solution, with a very caring but also professional attitude.

The D.O.C.T.O.R. As Our Role Model

Now that we know what our goal is (to redefine sales), and now that we are on the same page, it is time to get into the nuts and bolts of this system. The I HATE Selling sales process is broken down into six simple steps (D-O-C-T-O-R).

These steps were not just thought up because they were catchy or fun, they are the actual steps that the top Rainmakers in every field across the world use (whether they realize they are doing it or not). And you can apply them to your business today. This is the very same process that grew my business to well over six figures in less than three years! Get ready, because we are diving right in!

> **D** – Do they know that I care?
> **O** – Ouch! Where is the pain?
> **C** – Committed or just complaining?
> **T** – Top dollar?
> **O** – Outside influences?
> **R** – Real results and real referrals!

This is your chance to become The Rainmaker. This is where your attitude change meets your system and allows you the freedom to truly become creative in all that you do. There is no more hoping someone will want to train with you, wishing that someone will walk in the door and sign up for a new membership, no longer coming to the end of your pitch and being met with the dreaded awkward silence before you ask "So...would you like to sign up?" Or, maybe worse, never getting to the place that you can try and close the deal just because you think you know the answer is "No" before you even get the chance to ask the question. This model changes everything.

Over the next six chapters we will dive into exactly how to implement each step of the I HATE Selling sales process into your training business. From the first time you meet someone, to them bringing you clients and selling for you. In order to do this, we will take snapshots from real-life situations and show you how each type of trainer responds. I will introduce you to three friends of mine: Freddy Faker, Timmy Taker, and of course The Rainmaker. This is your chance to learn from their mistakes, to insert yourself into the story, to feel the pain and uncomfortableness of doing it all wrong, and then learn how to become just like The Rainmaker. You will find Freddy Faker often doing what Fakers do, making excuses and faking their way along. You will see Timmy Taker doing exactly what Takers do, pushing for more and making mistakes while they try and take all that they can for themselves. And finally The Rainmaker will show you what it looks like to work within this system to truly serve and connect with those around you.

Now remember, you will likely find yourself acting or thinking just like Freddy Faker and Timmy Taker quite often (especially if you are being honest with yourself). But, just because this is who you have been does not mean that this is who you forced to always be. Every single example used in this book comes from real world experiences that I have witnessed and many I have participated in! Many of the men and women from these examples have been on teams that I have run, worked side by side with, or even led me when I was first starting out. You can learn something about yourself from all of them and you can develop this system in your business by looking at the good, the bad, and the ugly, and being brutally honest with yourself. Let's learn from our mistakes so that we won't have to go through them again. Get a leg up now so that you won't experience the same problems later on.

Within Each Step You Will Find The Following…

> **The Goal:** What are you trying to accomplish in this step of the process?
>
> **The Why:** Why is this important?
>
> **The Scenario:** What does this look like in a real-life sales & training experience?
>
> **The Response:** How do Freddy Faker, Timmy Taker, and The Rainmaker respond?
>
> **The Challenge:** What are you personally going to do from here?

I will also ask you to take it a step further and ask you to…

Think Like A Rainmaker: Change the way you think and you change the way you act.

And we will continue to...

Put In The Work: It can't stop in these pages. Take it into your world.

Don't forget, you may very well be just like Freddy Faker in one scenario, Timmy Taker in the very next, and then turn around and be just like the Rainmaker in another. Don't be too quick to label yourself and box yourself into one category. It can be self-defeating. It will stop you from opening up your mind to see how you can change in other ways and in other scenarios. It can also stop your momentum of change. Be honest and real with yourself, whether it is positive or negative.

One final thought before we begin: this is the one time you can make this about you, not the people around you. If you run a team that needs this or if you have friends that you know deal with these issues, go through the system yourself first before you bring it to them. Once you've gone through it, then you can start to coach them in this process. When they see how it is affecting your attitude and your business, then they will give you the platform to help them. If you can come at this with an attitude of self-reflection, with the intention of bettering yourself no matter where you are, and work hard to apply this system to your personality and your style, then you will see everything around you begin to change.

Part 2 - Get Set!

Chapter 6 - Step 1
Do They Know That I Care?

THE GOAL

Start a meaningful relationship with someone you hardly even know.

THE WHY

Deep down we all know that relationships are where everything starts. As much as we try and make it about our excellent workouts, all of our credentials, education, and experience (and these things can be very important), the simple truth remains – if they don't know you, like you, and trust you, nothing else matters.

THE SCENARIO

Gary Getinshape is looking for a gym and a personal trainer to help him get back in shape. He knows that he needs help and doesn't want to injure himself. Money is not an issue. He has spent his life working, making money, and neglecting his health, and now he is finally ready to get his priorities in order. He makes the call to your facility because he heard about it from one of his friends. The phone rings, after you answer you hear Gary say, "Hello, I'd like to get some information on personal training." What do you do? What do you say? How would you respond?

Let's take a look at how Freddy Faker, Timmy Taker, and The Rainmaker respond:

THE RESPONSE

Freddy Faker

"Yeah? Sure, what would you like to know?"

- Well, How much is it?

"Our price that corporate sets is $65/session."

- Oh, ok. I guess I'm not exactly sure how that works...

"Yeah, I understand. It's a little pricey, but like I said, I don't really set the prices."

- Well if there is nothing that you can do about it I guess I could just come in and...

"OR, you know what?! Every so often we have a sale on training. That would be your best bet to save a little extra."

- Ok, I guess that works. When does that happen?

"Not for another three or four months usually. If you want to check back then, we can talk about it more."

- Well, I don't know if that will really work.

"Yeah it's not that great of a discount anyway and it takes so long to get here. Iif you change your mind let me know."

- I know, I just...

"Well let me know in a couple months if you want to try it out. Have a nice day. Bye."

Click.

Freddy Faker gets off the phone and thinks to himself, "Man, some people just don't get it. This is just a slow day. I wish I could find some people that really wanted a trainer."

What Happened Here???

You might say this is a little extreme, but this happens every single day. I've seen it dozens of times. Freddy Faker assumed that Gary needed a deal and he didn't take the time to really get to know him. There were no questions, there was no follow up, there was just Freddy Faking his way through the day and making excuses for everything that wasn't handed right to him, even when it was!

Gary picks up the phone again and tries another gym. The phone rings, after you answer, you hear Gary say, "Hello, I'd like to get some information on personal training..."

Timmy Taker

"Sure thing! I can get you in soon. I can really help you gain some muscle mass, we have some great plans and big discounts if you buy a membership today, but today is the last day for those promotions."

- I'm just wonder...

"You know what pal? I have time this afternoon to get you in, but make sure it's before 4:00 because that's when my shift ends and you don't want to work with the next guy who is coming on after me."

- But I'm thi-

"Look man we all have things we need to work on and I'm sure that's why you're calling, so let's get this started and rolling. If it's the money, just think about how much your morning donuts and coffee are costing you. Just think about those fast food lunches and dinners! And can you really afford the doctor's bills if you don't get in shape? Here's the deal, let's get you in and get you started today, I'll even cut 10% off the top when you sign up. I mean, come on, you want to play with your kids and grandkids without getting tired right? Or worse, you want to be around to see them grow up don't you?!"

Click.

Timmy Taker gets off the phone amazed at what Gary will be missing out on, and even more, the money that he will be saving. "What a loser, some people are just going to be fat forever, these people. I tell you what… who's next?"

What Happened Here???

Again, you might say this is out there, but I've seen worse. Timmy Taker did what Takers do. He didn't listen, he assumed too much, thought that he had all the answers, and never established any type of relationship with Gary Gettinshape. Without a meaningful relationship it doesn't matter what kind of advice or strategy Timmy Taker uses, it's not going to work.

Frustrated and ready to give up, Gary picks up the phone again and tries one last athletic club. The phone rings, after you answer, you hear Gary say, "Hello, I just need some info on personal training…"

The Rainmaker

"Yes sir, I can do that for you, what was your name?"

- Gary Gettinshape.

"Gary, I'm the Rainmaker, great to speak with you. How can I help you today?"

- I guess I just need to know how much it costs.

"Well Gary, we have a few different options for our training clients. Why don't you start by telling me a little about yourself and your situation and that way I can make sure I am guiding you in the right direction."

- Ok, I guess I just need to lose a little weight, ya know? I haven't been in a gym in a long time and I don't really know what to do.

"Sounds like a lot of people I've worked with."

- So you think there is hope for me?

"Gary, there is hope for everyone. Why don't we schedule a time to meet face-to-face where we can talk a little more and figure out exactly what you need and how we are going to get you there."

- That sounds great, I can't wait. I really appreciate you taking the time to just listen to me. You wouldn't believe what I've been through with some other gyms. I almost just gave up completely. I'm glad I found you.

"I'm glad you didn't give up either Gary. We'll figure out exactly what you need and make sure we are doing what is best for you."

- Thanks, I'm pretty free on Thursday. Do you have any time that afternoon?

"Thursday at 4:00 would be perfect if you can fit it in. We'll get you on the right path from here on out!"

- See you at 4:00. Thanks Rainmaker!

"Thank you Gary. I will see you then!"

What Happened Here???

How did the Rainmaker make such a quick connection? It's amazing what can happen when you take a minute to just stop and listen to someone.

Rainmakers ask the right questions to let those around them in order to show them these three things:

> They are more interested in serving them than just making a sale.

They are more interested in serving them than serving themselves.

They are more interested in serving them than anything else at that moment.

This is what builds trust and makes long lasting relationships. People know that you truly care when you listen and act like you are listening.

THE CHALLENGE

If there is one thing to take away from this chapter, here it is: learn to listen. Pick at least one of the following keys to becoming a better listener and start applying it today.

6 Keys to Becoming a Better Listener...

1. **Take notes.** Don't think about what you will say next, just listen and take notes. Always take notes. Resist the urge to say everything you want or need to say and ask questions to get to know them better. Your first goal is to speak just enough to keep the conversation going and keep it all about them. You need to understand who they are and they need to know that you care.

2. **Get them talking.** Be engaged. Act like everything they say is the most important thing ever. Let them know that you know what they are saying is important by physically listening with verbal and visual signals – nod your head, lean forward, say "uh-huh," "I see." The more they talk, the more they will like you. And the more you are physically interested in them, the more they will talk.

3. **Be curious.** Deal with imprecise responses. For example, "I'm consistent with my workouts." "I do cardio fairly often." "My diet is ok, better than most." Get them to be specific and give you details. Ask questions like, "How often is that?" "Why is that?" "What happened there?" Get them to expand their answers and

open up to you. If they won't, chances are they don't believe that you truly care yet.

4. **Get to know them.** Be interested in them – their business, their lives, their interests. Ask questions to prove it. Leave your fliers behind. Get to know the person you are talking to first. Now is not the time to sell. Besides, no one cares how good your marketing material is. A flier at the wrong time just says, "I don't care enough to listen, so you should read this." More than anything they need to know that you care for them. People don't want to feel like they are being sold to or just plugged into your system. They want to feel like they are receiving individualized care. The great thing here is that this is exactly what your system can be.

5. **Be yourself.** Let the buyer meet the real you. Be open and vulnerable. It's only when you are being yourself that you will allow the person across from you to open up and in turn be their true self as well. If you want to make a connection with someone they need to get to know the real you. If you are faking it, so will they. This is not an excuse to be weird or inappropriate. You can be professional and real at the same time. You have a lot to offer, but they need to know you first.

6. **Be patient.** Don't answer unasked questions. Wait to solve their problems later once you have gotten to the real issue. Get to what they care about. If you are not patient you will sound just like all other sales people. Write down thoughts and questions for later, if you spend time thinking about what is next, clients will know. Don't use a flier to sell – they may start paying more attention to it than to you. Send brochures or fliers afterwards when you follow up with a thank you note. Don't interrupt – not even if they are off topic.

4 Ways To Kill A Relationship Before It Begins…

These apply both when you're talking with someone face-to-face and when someone sees you from a distance.

1. **Your body language.** From the way you hold your arms, the way you present yourself, and the direction you look while you speak, your body speaks louder than anything you could ever say.

   Freddy Faker: "I am usually relaxed and leaning back, or crouched down I guess. I don't really think about it."

   Timmy Taker: "Power stance, power stare, leaning in, pointing, and engaging them. I'm going to make them see my point."

   The Rainmaker: "I am always confident in what I am doing, but I am careful not to overpower anyone. Hands on hips or behind my back at times. I often speak with my hands but am careful not to point aggressively. I want them to feel comfortable with me and be able to open up and at the same time know that I am an authority on the subject."

2. **Your appearance.** Think about everything about your outer appearance. How is your hair? Your eyes? Your clothes? Your breath? This may sound silly or simple or even shallow, BUT others are making snap judgments the moment they see you. Whether it is fair or not, they decide whether they like you or not within the first seven seconds.

   Freddy Faker: "I just woke up and rushed here because I didn't want to be late. It's not a big deal that I'm wearing the same shirt from yesterday. I can tuck it in later and wrinkles don't matter. I'll just grab a stick of gum and I'll be fine. It's up to them if they buy anything from me anyway."

   Timmy Taker: "I'm aggressive and ready to go – scented body wash, scented deodorant, cologne, axe spray. I look and smell better than anyone on the planet."

   The Rainmaker: "I'm in uniform, alert, and ready to go. Teeth brushed, hair nice, even had a mint after lunch to make sure my breath is still nice. I know everything I do outwardly is effecting the influence I can have on someone and help them."

3. **Your thoughts.** Thoughts lead to beliefs, beliefs lead to actions, actions lead to habits, habits form your lifestyle. It all starts with a thought. Renew your mind and don't let it rule you. In a sales or training situation if you are thinking about something else, you are not entirely focused on the person in front of you and they can tell.

   Freddy Faker: "I wouldn't say that I get distracted easily but there is always so much else going on around me. I mean my phone, the TVs, other members, other trainers, my boss might walk by, that girl I am always talking to."

   "I guess it all depends on how the day is going – slow day or good day, if I'm lucky or unlucky…"

   Timmy Taker: "I'm fully focused all the way. This person in front of me is going to make me some money, and then I'm going to get that next couple that just walked in signed up. I can probably push them together into a training group. Oh there is the guy who said he wanted to join the group too. Hold on a second, I'm going to get him over here too. I'll be right back."

   The Rainmaker: "I'm focused on who I am with right now and what they need the most. If I take excellent care of them, I know they will become raving fans and my business will grow the right way. Is today a lucky day? I don't believe in lucky days, nor do I believe in unlucky days or slow days for that matter – I work hard and prepare for the future. I am going to reap what I sow."

4. **Your Words and Tone of Voice.** If you are excited to be here they will be too. If you speak about your shift, your day, your business, this building as if you don't like it, guess who else won't like it and won't like you either?

Freddy Faker: "I make my calls, read the script, and get my work done when I can."

Timmy Taker: "I don't care what it takes, I just need to show them that I am right and they are wrong."

The Rainmaker: "I'm excited to talk to anyone I can help. I've found smiling helps a ton. If I am happy and excited to be here, they will be too. They want to be in a place where they can get away from negativity and manipulation, and I want to provide that."

Think Like A Rainmaker...

I will learn to listen. This is a skill I intentionally practice every single day.

Put In The Work...

Start up a conversation with anyone, think of this as training. Your goal is not to sell anything, but to practice listening and showing them that you care about them. See how long you can keep them talking and keep them interested by asking them questions and using some of the tools found in this chapter. Write down your experience below.

_____

_____

_____

_____

_____

_____

_____

_____

_____

For The Bold...

Sit down and think about what happened in your conversation. What did you do well? What was the hardest part? What tendencies do you feel surging up from the inside trying to ruin what you are working on? Message me your successes and failures: www.facebook.com/TrainingWithRyan

Chapter 7 - Step 2
Ouch! Where's The Pain?

THE GOAL

Find out what they really need and want.

THE WHY

You can have the best workouts in the world and be the best coach on the planet but if you don't know what someone needs, you can't help them and they won't buy from you. You become just another workout generator, another YouTube channel, another magazine article promising great results but not taking the time to know what those result should actually be. Now is the time to ask great questions and dig deep.

THE SCENARIO

Mary Moveit, a relatively healthy looking lady walks up to the trainer's desk. She says, "I really need to get a trainer. My friend said you guys were pretty good here, but I just really need someone to show me what to do and how to do it." What do you do? What do you say? How would you respond?

Let's take a look at how Freddy Faker, Timmy Taker, and the Rainmaker respond.

THE RESPONSE

Freddy Faker

"Oh thanks. I'm glad your friend thought that. Yeah that machine over there is probably the best, but then you could also do this one for cardio and we have some classes that are good too."

- Ok, sounds good, I've been kind of doing some of those machines and I use the treadmill like you said. I guess I just need some help, I'm feeling like I need something more.

"Oh no, you're doing great, just don't give up, you can do this.

- "Uh, ok... thanks...

"Sure thing, have a great day, let me know if you need anything else..."

What Happened Here???

Freddy Faker went straight for the advice – and not very good advice at that. And here's the thing to remember – it could be the best advice in the world, the best training tip of all time, but if they are not ready to hear it, that great advice becomes worthless. Freddy Faker couldn't see that Mary's problem was not just surface level encouragement or what machine to use, but something deeper. Why? Because he never asked.

If you cannot find out what their biggest need is, if you cannot find their pain, you'll never be able to relate to them and you surely won't be able to inspire them. You'll be just like Freddy Faker, faking your way through another day, confused as to why you don't have enough clients to work with and why the ones you do have don't change.

Timmy Taker

"Perfect. Here's the deal, I have time tomorrow and we can get you on some incline sprints to get your metabolism firing the way it should, and then we will start some high intensity circuits. This is what will work for you especially since you're trying to burn off that extra fat from your last baby, am I right? It should take about 25 sessions to get through that for starters and that'll cost $2,250. But if you can start tomorrow I can get you a nice discount. How about 3:00 pm?"

- Well, I guess. I was sort of...

"Look, you can do this, it will be perfect. We have a lot of work to do but you can make it happen. Just think, if that girl over there can do it, so can you."

- That's not what I'm asking at all. I don't think you understand.

"Sure I understand, but you need to understand that this is a commitment. Are you ready to do this or not?"

- No, not at all. I'll just find someone else.

"Fine. Suit yourself." (Her loss anyway.)

What Happened Here???

Timmy Taker is off and running again. Constantly in his own world, he cannot see that there is a real person in front of him, not just a dollar sign. And unfortunately, he could actually be a decent trainer if he would just slow down and ask the right questions, but he won't, because all he does is take.

If you are too quick to tell them their biggest need, and their worst pain, you'll never connect. It has to be THEIR need and THEIR pain. You'll end up just like Timmy Taker, either overwhelming your clients with your constant pushing for more or mad at them for not committing. This ruins their experience and your reputation.

The Rainmaker

"Wow Mary, that is great to hear! Who was it? I love knowing we've helped someone."

- It was a good friend of mine, Jane Justajogger. She just had a few kids and life got in the way and she said you helped her turn it all around.

"Yes! Jane! Do you know what is so special about Jane? She is determined. She just got tired of settling for the same old thing and that's when I met her. She works so hard, I'm so glad she is inspiring others too! I'll have to say something to her. In fact, her next session is on me."

- You're right she is and she does, you seem to really care about her. And that's so great that you are giving her a free session, she has really inspired me a lot.

"That's great to hear Mary, and yes, I like to reward my clients for inspiring others. Now, how can I help you?"

- I am just having trouble, and it seems silly, but I want to be able to do a real push up and feel like an athlete.

"You know what, that is a really common issue that many of the people I work with have when they are first starting with me. It's actually really impressive that you noticed and want to do something about it. How did you realize that your pushups weren't great?"

-Honestly, I noticed the changes Jane has been making and I realized that I'm not where I'd like to be.

"Well, let me tell you a secret. Jane has worked really hard on her pushups too and she was feeling the exact same way when we started. She changed a lot about her routine, and now she is getting some incredible results."

- That's what she said, and that's why I'm here.

"That's great! You know, I believe, everyone has an athlete inside of them ready to be revealed. Have you played many sports in the past?"

- Just soccer and volleyball in high school but that was so long ago. I guess I just don't feel like I move right anymore.

"I know that can be a big issue – once you feel like you can't do it right, you just don't want to do it anymore and it becomes that much harder to start back again. It turns into this huge cycle, and it feels like it gets worse and worse and worse."

- Yeah, exactly! And my sister and my husband are in like crazy good shape and I just had a kid a year ago. I mean, I've always ran a little or did machines to stay in shape but it just hit me that I can't really do what they can do. I feel like they are in a club that I can't really be a part of anymore. I just don't know what to do.

"You know what? You are going to do it. We can break that cycle today. There really is no secret club, in fact the club is this, people like you who are tired of the path they are on and decide to make a change. And that's exactly what we are going to do."

- (With a huge smile on her face.) Sounds good to me, where do we start?

"We just did Mary. Now that we know why we are doing this, we can set a time to do our initial evaluation and talk about what's needed from there. What does tomorrow look like for you?"

What Happened Here???

How was the Rainmaker able to make such a deep connection? Once someone knows that you care about them, you're on the right path. But you can't stop there. Go back and look how the Rainmaker navigates the conversation and finds out exactly where Mary's pain is. It wasn't just encouragement, it really had nothing to do with the price, it wasn't even her pushups or outward needs. It was something much different. Mary felt left out, ashamed, rejected. She wanted more than anything to be accepted by her sister, she wanted to feel wanted by her husband. This could be the beginning to helping them find themselves and who they really feel they were meant to be which is what this is all about in the long run. And Freddy Faker and Timmy Taker think it's just about working out!

Once you've found their pain, you can start to relate to them and that means that you can start to help them. Relationship is not enough, but it was necessary for them to open up and share what they are really dealing with on the inside. Now you can start to evaluate and see what they need from you during your sessions.

THE CHALLENGE

We all want to be in control during the sales process. We all want to feel like we are the ones directing the sale and making it go well. We are all scared that if we let go of control, the sale and our potential client will unravel and disappear before our very eyes. But, we cannot be ruled by fear. Here is the problem with trying to hold on to control – the person potentially buying from you also wants control. They are terrified of getting ripped off and they aren't sure they can even handle this new adventure they are getting into. If you play the control game it means that one of you has to win and one of you has to lose. This is not a "win-win" scenario. In step 1 "Do They Know that I Care?" we very simply and carefully learned to listen. In step 2 "Ouch! Where is the Pain?" we continue listening and now start asking questions. The best questions get the best answers. Let them talk and let them lead the conversation. It might seem like you are giving away your control, but you are not. Remember: it is ok if they talk more than you. In fact, that is exactly what you want to draw out of them. If you can ask the right questions and honestly listen, you will find yourself in control of the conversation.

> If you are not asking the right questions, you are wasting your time.
>
> If you are not asking the right questions, you cannot help anyone.
>
> If you are not asking the right questions, you are losing control.

Remember back to a time when you were...

Wasting your time or someone else's.

Not able to help someone.

Not in control.

3 Things To Remember When Looking For Pain...

1. **Give up control.** The person who is asking the questions is the one in control of the conversation.

    Freddy Faker: "I let them take control, I don't want to be manipulative."

    Timmy Taker: "I take the control, they need to know what I want them to know."

    The Rainmaker: "I ask questions and let them talk. I can always bring it back around with another good question."

2. **Hold off on price.** Money is almost never the reason someone won't buy for you – they just use it to justify their feelings. This is not the time to convince them of your price, it is the time to find out what they truly care about.

    Freddy Faker: "I just answer the questions they ask me."

    Timmy Taker: "I make sure they can pay right away, I don't like wasting time."

    The Rainmaker: "I ask the right questions to make sure I am helping them properly."

3. **Use what you have.** You have two ears and one mouth, use them in the proportion they were given to you. If you are talking more

than 33% of the time during the selling process, you are talking too much.

Freddy Faker: "I'll do what I can if someone asks my advice on something."

Timmy Taker: "They need to know what I know, I have to be the one to tell them.

The Rainmaker: "I know the person asking the right questions and listening is always in a place to help and lead."

Think Like A Rainmaker…

This is more than working out, I am dealing with deep seeded emotions that may take some time to heal. I will ask the right questions and help people find their true motivations.

Put In The Work…

What are the right questions to find their pain?

Prepare 20 questions that dig into the heart of "why" so you can be prepared at a moment's notice to help anyone.

1. _____

2. _____

3. _____

4. _____

5. _____

6. _____

7. _____

8. _____

9. _____

10. _____

11. _____

12. _____

13. _____

14. _____

15. _____

16. _____

17. _____

18. _____

19. _____

20. _____

For The Bold...

Go right now and use these questions with anyone that knows that you do truly care – maybe even the person you randomly started a conversation with in "Step 1 - Do They Know That I Care?" This can be tough if you aren't used to it. Let me know what kind of feedback you receive: www.facebook.com/TrainingWithRyan

Chapter 8 - Step 3 Committed or Just Complaining?

THE GOAL

Find out if they are serious about making a change.

THE WHY

People can have all the pain in the world, they can know that they need to change, BUT unless they are committed to doing something about it, nothing will ever change. At this step you are looking for those who are ready to make the commitment to following your advice instead of those who just want to take up all of your time.

THE SCENARIO

A regular member to your gym, Charlie ChestDay, walks in while you are working and says "Hi." You see Charlie every day and you two get along great. Over the past few weeks he has been complaining of some discomfort in his back but seems a little different today. He walks up to the desk and says, "This pain really isn't going away, and to top it off I am plateauing on my bench. Maybe I just need some rest, then I can get back to it even harder, what do you think?" What do you do? What do you say? How would you respond?

Let's take a look at how Freddy Faker, Timmy Taker, and The Rainmaker respond.

THE RESPONSE

Freddy Faker

"Charlie, yeah man, that's no fun. I hope that back feels better, it sounds like you need to rest it. Let me know if you need anything else."

- Thanks Freddy, we'll see how it goes…

"I wish there was something I could do for you Charlie."

- Me too Freddy…

"Have a great day."

What Happened Here???

Freddy Faker has the relationship and Charlie "knows that he cares." And in this instance there is actual, real pain. Something needs to be done, but what did Freddy Faker do? He did what Faker's always do, he made excuses. He didn't go deep enough, he didn't ask, didn't listen, he cares more about being comfortable with people than helping them. Too often we just let our time and our opportunities slip through our fingers, time that we could be helping people instead of just commiserating with them. The Fakers of the world usually have trouble finding someone's commitment level simply because they don't go deep enough. They are great with relationships on the surface, they are great with others opening up and finding their pain, but they have trouble finding committed clients.

Timmy Taker

"Come on Chuck don't be chump, you can push through this. Let me show you something that will help you out right now."

- I don't know, do you really think it's alright?

"It's all in your head man, break through the barrier, power on. Tell you what, first tip is on me and then we'll do some sessions to really get things growing."

- Alright, you're the expert, let's try it out.

"That's what I'm talking about!"

What Happened Here???

Timmy Taker is about to make the sale! But let's look at what is really going on here. It happens almost too quickly, and there is no real commitment on Charlie ChestDay's part at all. This has all the makings of disaster. If you want clients who quit after just a couple sessions, clients who feel guilty, clients who never really open up to what their true goals are, then sell this way. But you better get used to doing it often because this is the path to high turnover. Look at what Timmy Taker did here, it is exactly what Taker's always do… he took advantage, he didn't ask, didn't listen, he cares more about what he can get out of the person than how he can help them.

For some people it can seem simple to build a relationship with someone (at least on the surface). The Timmy Takers of the world are great at starting that phony surface level relationship and it seems so good! But it comes crashing down so quickly. The commitment needs to be Charlie's not just yours. When you focus all of the energy toward yourself, you completely forget about the reason you are actually there in the first place, to help and serve people just like Charlie ChestDay. Let's hope he doesn't get seriously hurt along the way…

The Rainmaker

"Charlie, I'm so sorry to hear that your back is still bothering you. How long has it been?"

-You know, I'm not 100% sure. I feel like it's maybe been 2-3 weeks or so. It's just nagging and needs to get better, I figured this is the best way to get over it. Then I have this high school reunion coming soon, so I want to get back and lift even harder after this is gone.

"Hmmm, have you considered that it might be the way that you are training that is affecting your back?"

- Well yeah but that's why I'm going to take a break."

"Of course, but knowing how hard you work and that you have this reunion coming up, it seems to me that when you come back in, you'll do the same routine that got you in this mess. And you'll likely lift even heavier and harder trying to make up for lost time and not only hurt yourself but it could leave you barely moving for your reunion."

- Man, I never thought of it like that. Now that you mention it, I have dealt with this before.

"You know, if you'd like some help fine tuning your training program to make sure it is helping you move better AND getting the results your looking for, that's what I do. A lot of my clients have found great gains by adding a few progressions to their programs. It can be tough to switch things up but the results are real. If you're really wanting to change we can talk more about it."

-That would be great, I can't believe I never saw this before. This could change everything.

"If you're serious about this, we can set a time to meet in a week to plan this out. That will give your body the break it needs to recover and give you time to get checked out, then we can build a new program and get you ready for that reunion."

-Sound good, let's do that. I need to make a change.

What Happened Here???

How was the Rainmaker able to find their true commitment? Did you notice how easy this conversation was? You can almost see yourself saying it. Did you see how easy it was for the Rainmaker to ask deep questions? To find commitment we often need to dig a little deeper. You have listened, you have asked, and now you are nailing them down on their real commitments. We can get so caught up in trying to make the sale that we forget to simply and honestly find out about the person standing right in front of us. The Rainmakers of the world know one main thing, "It's not about me." It's not about how good I am or even how much I can obviously help them. It is about them – what they need, why they need it and, as we saw in this example, when they need it by. You cannot force someone to change BUT you can inspire them. Here is the trick – inspiration has nothing to do with your great conquests and feats, but it has everything to do with allowing them to see what they can conquer and defeat. To help them realize where they could be!

Sure, your experience or expertise might be what originally attracts someone to you. Maybe it's your great body or insane strength, and the fact that they want to be like you. Maybe you have the most creative workouts and get amazing results, and they want them too. BUT, those things are not truly inspiring. Rainmakers know they can turn the interest someone else has in them into a belief that person has in themselves.

You have this ability in you, it just needs to be sharpened. Think about the most influential, inspiring people you know. It's very rarely what they have done that inspires you, it is the way they make you feel when you are around them. They bring out the best in you, now you can go and bring out the best in others.

THE CHALLENGE

We must learn to test for commitment. As you are following through the D.O.C.T.O.R. steps, here are three mental check points to take note of to see if your potential client is committed or just complaining.

>Do they speak openly and freely? If not, go back to step 1.

>Are they emotionally involved? If not, go back to step 2.

Are they committed to this? Why? Why not? If not, go back and ask better questions.

2 Quick Ways To Test Their Commitment...

1. **Search for the Signs** – Listen for times they may be willing to get going – starting dates, anniversaries, trips, seasons, vacations, deadlines.

    Freddy Faker: "Well, here is something that will help you..."

    Timmy Taker: "I have time today, let's get started right now."

    The Rainmaker: Listens early for signs of commitment and brings them back up at the right time in the conversation.

2. **Ask.** Just flat out ask them if they are serious about making a change. But do it correctly.

    Freddy Faker: "Just let me know when you want to start."

    Timmy Taker: "Do you really want to be the way you are forever?!"

    The Rainmaker: "How important is this to you?" "When would you like to see this change?" "How serious are you about making this change?

This is just the start. As you begin to test others commitment levels more and more you will find yourself wasting less and less time with people who were never going to buy in the first place. Start picking up these signs early on. You are working hard to discover how much they will allow you to help them. Remember, nothing will work better than your own words delivered the proper way at the proper time.

Think Like A Rainmaker...

People can have all the pain in the world but unless they are willing to do something about it, nothing will ever change. I will help them find what they are truly committed to.

Put In The Work...

You have done the work for yourself of finding your "Why" when we started this book, now go and help 5 others find their "Why." What is important to them will guide you to where they are committed. Their "Why" is more important to them than your "Why." Record your experience and what you found out about them and yourself through this exercise here.

1. _____

_____

_____

_____

_____

2. _____

_____

_____

_____

_____

3. _____

_____

_____

_____

_____

4. _____

_____

_____

_____

_____

5. _____

_____

_____

_____

_____

For The Bold...

This is big, you need to be able to reach beyond the surface if you want to inspire people. If you can inspire, if you can motivate, you can help people truly change. Knowing the obstacles that are in someone's way can be a very helpful thing. What are some of the objections that you commonly hear? There is a solution and there is likely something much deeper that needs to be addressed for each one. Take that step and go deeper, find their real commitment level and don't just settle for the first answer they give you. Then let me hear about it: www.facebook.com/TrainingWithRyan

Chapter 9 - Step 4
Top Dollar?

THE GOAL

Find out if they are willing to pay what you are worth.

THE WHY

You want to spend your time with the people who value what you do the most. We all deserve to be paid for what our services are worth.

THE SCENARIO

A young man who recognizes you as a personal trainer in your facility walks up and asks, "So how much is a session? What does training cost?" What do you do? What do you say? How would you respond?

Let's take a look at how Freddy Faker, Timmy Taker, and The Rainmaker respond.

THE RESPONSE

Freddy Faker

"Well... A one-hour training session generally costs $70 per hour and I know that's expensive. But, if you are really interested I can just take you through a couple workouts and write some stuff down for you to do on your own. I know the economy is rough and I can't expect you to pay that much every time. Or even better, I can just charge you my group rate and let you come one-on-one. I don't mind making less if it will help you out too..."

- No thanks, I'm looking for some real professional training. I don't think you are the right fit. I need someone who takes this seriously, is there anyone else around here I can talk with? I want a professional.

"Oh, um, ok. I guess I can find someone else for you if that's what you'd like..."

What Happened Here???

Freddy Faker doesn't feel comfortable talking about money. He thinks the reason he can't get any clients is because the economy is bad, people don't have money, or times are just tough. He is always out to help someone (or so he thinks) but no one ever truly values what he does so he can't seem to help anyone at all. He didn't want to come off as pushy or "salesy" and he hates to make people uncomfortable, especially himself. But what ultimately happens time and time again is that it makes everyone uncomfortable. He misses out on helping someone who was ready to commit to a real change in their life, all because he didn't bring up price at the proper time in the proper way.

Timmy Taker

"Yeah man, a training session is $70 per hour, unless you want to buy 10 then I can knock it down to $65. Or if you want to get rolling right away and go big with the 25 pack of sessions, I can knock another 10% off that. Tell you what, I have tomorrow morning open at 11:00 am. I can tell that you want to get in here and get working on those guns, am I right??"

- Well actually, I ...

"You know what? You're right we will start with the core and get that six-pack working. That's what it's all about, am I right? Just like this (Timmy lifts his shirt to show off his six-pack). I mean it's always beach season when you look like this right, right? You know what – bring a friend with you and it'll be win-win. I can cut you both a deal and I make a little more, nice bonus. Even better, get here at 12:00 and I will throw you in my group of guys. Get ready for a crazy work out man, they are wild. Here let me get the paperwork ready for you, have you decided if you want to do the 10 or 25 pack yet?

- No, no, NO! This is not what I want, or what I need, this is ridiculous! I'm done with this place.

What Happened Here???

All Timmy Taker ever c/ares about is his bottom line. Sure he will cut prices if it means getting a new client, but he doesn't seem to care about what that client needs. Which is somewhat sad in itself because if Timmy really cared about his bottom line and the cash he could make, he would take time to care about what his potential clients needed the most. You can tell that he values his time and what his training is worth, but he is missing one huge point. He doesn't value what his clients are worth. Wanting to make money is not his problem, but caring more about money than about his clients is.

The Rainmaker

"Well, we have a couple of different options, I can sure help you decide which one is the best fit for you. What's your name?"

- I'm Richie Rich

"Great to meet you Richie Rich, what exactly are you training for?"

- Well, I have had some injuries in the past and I need some help getting moving the right way again. I've never really lifted weights or anything before, but I know I need to take care of my body now. It's just been tough to find time, but now I'm ready to make the time. I work a lot so it would have to be early in the morning but I want this to be a new routine for me, something I get up and start my day with every day.

"That's a great attitude to have Richie. Sorry to hear about those injuries, what exactly have you injured and does it still bother you?"

- It was more my back than anything else. I had a herniated disc and my neck was hurting too. But they are both much better now and I'm cleared by the doc. I'm just hunched over a computer all day and driving all over town for meetings. I just need a change.

"Richie, you are far too young to be having those kind of issues. The stress of your job and the position it has you in has to be tough. I'm glad to see that you are taking this seriously. It sounds like you are ready to really do something about it."

- I really am, I never want to feel that way again. Plus, I know my dad did the same thing. He worked hard, made money, made time for our family too, but he never really took care of himself. I really saw it take a toll on his body. He was in pain up until the end of his life. I don't want to put my family through that, or myself for that matter!

"I don't want you to either, but you need to realize this isn't a quick fix. You've spent years beating yourself up, we are really going to have to get serious to relieve it and move past what's been done. Do you understand?"

- Definitely, I know it won't be easy but I'm in, I'm ready to go. What's the next step?

"Let's set up your evaluation and get you in my schedule. That first session will last an hour and then I can give you a much better idea of what program you'll need to be on from there. I have time Monday, Tuesday, Thursday and Friday at 6:00 am. We will need to start with a lot of corrective work and then as your body progresses we will work on building other areas of focus and maintaining all that you've gained so that you don't start breaking yourself down again. We can evaluate on Monday and slowly build from there. Do those days and times work for you?"

-That sounds perfect, I'll be here Monday morning. Can I charge it to my card?

"Sure thing, I'll put you in my schedule right now. The first session will be $90 for the evaluation. Once you get fully evaluated and screened I will be able to tell you exactly where you'll need to be and what program to put you on. From our conversation today, it seems like we will need to start you on my 12-week Corrective Program, but we will let the screen decide where you begin. We won't know how that back has hindered you until then."

- That's great, I love how comprehensive this is. I can't wait to get in for the evaluation. This is exactly what I have needed. Everywhere else I have been to just wants to make me lift like I am training for the Olympics or a body building competition. This is going to be so much better. What will the cost likely be once we get rolling?

"If we end up doing the 12-week Corrective Program, four times/week, it will cost $3,840. That's me with you four days a week for 12 weeks. Of course I will require you to do some homework and stretches on the off-days if we are really going to conquer this."

- Sounds like this is exactly what I need, here's my card.

"I'll get it set up for you right now and as you progress we will constantly be re-evaluating and re-assessing where you are and where you need to be."

- I love it. I'm ready.

What Happened Here???

How was The Rainmaker able to get him on board with his price? The Rainmaker asked questions and waited for the perfect time to bring up price. Even when directly asked "How much is a session?" he still brilliantly answered with a question because it is impossible to know who you are talking to and what they specifically need until you get to know them.

Once he knew who he was talking to, the Rainmaker wasn't afraid to offer his best. You might be thinking, "But won't offering four days a week be too much for most people?" Yes, it might be. But, most people are not Richie Rich and most trainers are not Rainmakers. When you have a client that is in great need, is strongly committed, is willing and able to pay top dollar, you offer them your very best option.

If I pull up to the nicest steakhouse in town in my brand new Maserati, ready for my reservation at my privately reserved table, and the waiter offers me a "dollar menu" and suggests the "deal of the day" trying to save me a few bucks, I would be insulted. I have come to the best place in town to get the best meal in town, at this point money is not an issue. I am always perfectly capable of saying, "No, that's too much." If I want the best and I can spend the best, I want to be offered the best. Show me the best bottle of wine, your most excellent cut of meat, the best things you have to offer. It is now an inconvenience to me if someone offers me anything less than the best, because they have just wasted my time. Why do we think it should be any different in our training or our memberships? Through just a brief conversation, the Rainmaker learned that Richie Rich needed "the best," and he wasn't afraid to offer it to him. Anything less, and Richie would be training somewhere else.

Remember, most people think in terms of good, better, and best. These thoughts are going through the minds of our clients and potential members every time they buy something, even if only on a subconscious level. It is important to be able to discern who you are talking with and at what level they typically think. There are times when it is necessary to let the prospective client feel like they are getting a good deal. BUT, it must be your decision, not just simply giving away something for nothing. This is how you stay in control of the sales process.

> **Good** - "I want something good, but I am not willing to pay much for it. I want to feel like I am getting something of quality for a good deal."
>
> **Better** - "I want an upgrade, I want something better than normal. I want to feel like I can get better things than most people can get, and I am willing to spend a little more to have them. But I am not quite ready to get the top of the line, full package."
>
> **Best** - "I want the absolute best product and service. I want to feel like I am getting an incredible experience out of everything

that I purchase. If you don't offer me your best, you've wasted my time."

Notice that when asked about price…

Freddy Faker was very timid, almost ashamed of the price, waits too long in the process to bring it up, if at all.

Timmy Taker was too pushy, brings up price too early before his prospective client is emotionally involved.

The Rainmaker makes sure the person was ready to hear the information they needed before speaking too much.

THE CHALLENGE

We often fall into the trap of "trying to save our clients' money" but if we were to be honest with ourselves, we really don't think we are worth the price we are asking. Or perhaps we are just uncomfortable talking about money. After all, you didn't become a personal trainer to sell. You need to get past that way of thinking right now. You must remember, everything is sales, but it does not have to be cheesy or disingenuous. If someone wants the best, give them the best and they will love you for it, even if they are paying more. Everything costs money, there is no reason to be embarrassed or shy about charging what you are worth.

3 Reasons To Test For Their Ability To Pay…

1. Avoid wasting time
2. Avoid unnecessary objections
3. Avoid negative momentum

It is important to bring up price early in the conversation, but not too early! You need to know what the need is before you can price out the solution. This isn't to say that your training price will change with every client, but if you don't know what they need how can telling them a price help?

Painting a big picture can inspire change, telling them a single session dollar amount makes it all about money. Far too often we walk into a situation where we are trying to sell training by the session because that is how we've priced it out in our heads and on our budget sheets. One hour of my time = X dollars of your money. We must stop speaking about training in terms of single session or group session prices and start to think about training in terms of results! No one wants to buy a five or ten pack of training. But who wouldn't want the energy to play with their grandkids? To have their wife look at them with desire once again? To be their son's super hero instead of the family couch potato?!

Go through the sales process properly. (1) Let them know you care, (2) find out what they truly need, (3) figure out how committed they are, (4) and show them that you are worth every single penny they are spending and so much more. Thinking about money properly changes the way you speak to your clients and potential members because you are all about results, not just a dollar amount per session. Simply giving someone a price does not help them make a proper decision. Take them through each step of the process.

Think Like A Rainmaker...

I know that potential clients are almost always willing to pay a higher fee if they are emotionally connected in the selling process. Price objections are almost always just a surface level excuses, masking the real concern.

Put In The Work...

Take some time to do an inventory here. What are the last 5 things you purchased? This could be anything from lunch to your latest phone, a new outfit to a new car. Think about the purchases and where your thoughts were when buying them. Were you thinking in terms of Good, Better, or Best? Knowing how you naturally think in buying situations will make you more aware of how others are thinking when you are in your next sales scenario. Write down your thoughts on the spaces below.

1. _____

2. _____

3. _____

4. _____

_____

_____

_____

_____

5. _____

_____

_____

_____

_____

For The Bold…

Change the way you talk about money. Find out if the people around you are 'good,' 'better,' or 'best' people. Go back to the list of five people that you helped find their "why" from "Step 2 - Committed or Just Complaining" and dig a little deeper into the conversation. Do they want what is the absolute best? What is a little better than normal? Or are they more of the mindset of finding something that is good for a good deal? Then let me hear about their response: www.facebook.com/TrainingWithRyan

Chapter 10 - Step 5 Outside Influences?

THE GOAL

Find out who is really making the final decision.

THE WHY

Knowing who is influencing your potential client and member can give you direction on who to speak with and how to speak to them, this will lead to long term client retention and strong referral sources.

THE SCENARIO

Kyle TheKid approaches you, his favorite trainer in the gym, and begins to tell you how much he wants to get ready for his high school basketball season.

- I'm so excited for this year, I think I have a real chance of starting! If I can just get my vertical jump up another couple of inches and get a step or two faster, I am set! I even talked to my dad and he said I can start training for it this summer but I only have two months until school starts back again! Will you train me? What do you do? What do you say? How would you respond?

Let's take a look at how Freddy Faker, Timmy Taker, and The Rainmaker respond.

THE RESPONSE

Freddy Faker

"Awesome Kyle! That is so exciting, I'm glad you are serious about taking your game to the next level. Of course I'll train you! I have time next week if you think that might work, or maybe the week after."

- Oh, ok.

"We can lift and play some basketball together, it'll be so much fun. Plus I'll get my work out in too."

- Yeah, that might be fun. But I was really wanting to train. I want to get better this year. I could have a chance at varsity! And then college! Who knows!?!

"Oh for sure! Don't worry about that at all. We will train. Don't worry buddy we'll do it together.»

- ...Uh, well, ok. I guess so... see you later...

What Happened Here???

Sure, Freddy cares about helping Kyle TheKid, but he again shows his lack of professionalism. In wanting to help, he doesn't listen. He assumes the kid is on his own and can't afford it, and he assumes incorrectly. Not only will he not help Kyle with his plan to train, but now he won't be able to help Kyle at all because he is likely going somewhere else to train with someone else. Not knowing who is influencing the buying decision here took away the chance for Freddy Faker to help someone in need, and that is exactly whom he claims to care the most about. His need to be comfortable and being seen as the "cool trainer" turned quickly into everyone around him thinking, "This guy obviously can't help me."

Timmy Taker

"Of course Kyle, but I need you to get serious with this. I'm talking 4-5 days a week, the whole summer, you don't miss a day! Are you ready for that?"

- Heck yes! That's exactly what I'm talking about!

"Ok, and your dad said it's ok?"

- Oh yeah, he loves the idea of me getting better and training for basketball. He wants me to do whatever it takes to get better.

"Perfect, then let's get going now. I'll talk with your dad later and get everything worked out with him. Can you have him call me?"

- Sure will. He's really busy but I will tell him to get ahold of you.

The following week, six sessions into an unpaid package of training...

"Kyle you're doing great, but I haven't heard from your dad yet, tell him to call me when he can, ok?"

- My dad said he is out of town this week but we are still good to go. He will be back soon and said he'd call you then and figure out a time to come in and pay.

"Ok, great! Sounds good. I'm keeping track so he can just pay all altogether once we talk. I don't want you to miss out until then."

A week later and now 10 sessions into an unpaid package...

"Kyle, your dad still hasn't called me. I need to talk to him tonight, this is getting ridiculous. Can I just have his number?"

- Sure thing, here it is...

Timmy Taker calls Kyle TheKid's father, DadInTheDark.

"Sir, I have been training your son Kyle for the past two weeks to help him get ready for basketball tryouts. He said it was ok with you and that you would pay for the package of sessions when you and I spoke. Would you like to do that now?"

- DadInTheDark – "HE DID WHAT!?!?!?! I never said that, there is no way! We talked about it being a possibility but his mother and I never gave the ok, which is why I haven't called you and which is why I haven't paid for anything! We decided that it wasn't in the budget for this summer. Is this how you run your business?? I can't believe this!

What Happened Here???

Did you notice how Timmy jumped right in, excited to get it going? You can't fault him for his enthusiasm but all he saw was dollar signs, thinking he has hit it big with a kid whose parents will pay for everything. But, since he didn't take the time to care about who was making the final decision, guess who doesn't get paid, and guess who gets grounded from the basketball team? We call this Lose-Lose and it had so much potential when it started. Timmy Taker is doing what he always does, taking where he can, just to help himself, and this time is has come back to bite him.

The Rainmaker

"Sure thing Kyle! I am so glad to see that you are getting serious about your game. Are your mom and dad on board with this?"

- Oh yeah, my dad loves the idea of me getting better and training for basketball. He wants me to do whatever it takes to get better.

"Perfect, is he around or should I just give him a call?"

- He isn't here today, but sure. I guess you can call him.

"Thanks Kyle, I just want him on the same page with us as well. Plus, he will be the one paying for the sessions, right?"

- Oh yeah, that's right, that makes sense. Here is his number.

"Thanks, I'll call him right now and then we can get started as soon as possible, ok?"

-OK! Thanks Rainmaker!

The Rainmaker, calls Kyle TheKid's father, Dad TheDecisionMaker and walks through the D.O.C.T.O.R. process with him as well because he knows that while Kyle TheKid will be his client, his Dad, the decision maker, has all the power because he will be writing the checks.

What Happened Here???

How was the Rainmaker able to get everyone on the same page? This started off great, he gave the time and respect to Kyle TheKid that he needed to feel special but also realized that he was likely not speaking to the true decision maker. By following the correct process, Rainmakers don't come across like robots who don't care nor do they get caught up in the excitement of a potential new sale. Getting in front of the decision maker is vital. It will often be the person who is also participating in the sessions being purchased, but there will be many times when there is something else going on behind the scenes.

THE CHALLENGE

You have shown them that (1) you really care, (2) you have found out where it really hurts, (3) you know they are committed and (4) able to pay. Now, (5) find out who makes the final decision.

Here are some great questions to ask yourself throughout the sales process to help you determine who the outside influencers are.

"Who are the decision makers here?" You want to know them.

"When will this decision be made?" You want to be there.

"How will this decision be made?" You need to know the way they think.

While you are asking yourself these questions it helps to know who you are dealing with. There are three types of influencers in this process. If you can identify them, you will be able to see what each one needs from you and from the others around them.

The Three Types of Influencers Behind Every Decision

1. **The Main Man** - the one who is actually using what you are offering. They will often act like they have the final say in the decision, but often they do not.

    Examples: Son, Daughter, Team, Elderly Parents/Grandparents, Coach, etc.

    Why you need them on your side: Provide these people with world class service and you have just created a fan for life who raves about you to everyone they are around.

2. **The Money Man** - the one who signs the checks, they will usually have the final say in the purchase. If not the final say, you can bet that their opinion will carry a lot of weight.

    Examples: Husband, Wife, Mom, Dad, CFO, AD, Head Coach, President, etc.

    Why you need them on your side: If they aren't sold, no one is buying.

3. **The Mob** - anyone collection of people leading your client, good or bad. This group is the most often overlooked but can have a huge impact, especially subconsciously. We often buy things or do things just because we believe it will make us look a certain way to a certain person or group of people.

    Examples: Friends, Parents, Siblings, Co-workers, Peers, etc.

Why you need them on your side: they often have strong influence with your potential client or sale and they can become your biggest ally.

The Importance Of Influence…

This is more than just dealing with young clients or minors. The example of Kyle TheKid hits home because it proves the point brilliantly and IT ACTUALLY HAPPENED!

It is so important to remember that the potential client in front of you has so many different influences in his or her life. Husband/wife, parent/child, friend/co-worker, etc. While not all of the relationships around them will directly affect their purchasing decision in that moment, they will always decide how your client feels about their purchase after they have bought. You want that feeling to be as pleasant as possible. Obviously, you cannot physically go to each potential relationship and convince them that this is a good thing for every single one of your clients. BUT, you can cover a ton of leg work up front if you follow this system properly and answer any objections that commonly come up.

This is the perfect time to bring their commitment level back up, and why they want to do this in the first place. You want them to take this new goal seriously, to start to look at their life a little more holistically, to realize that what they do outside the gym will affect the results inside the gym. Their sleep, their diet, their stress, their rest and recovery, it is all so important. If they don't have influencers in their life that are on your side it will be an uphill battle the whole way. Bring it up now, and lead them to the people who will be good influencers. Talk often of the importance of strong, positive influencers in their life. Trust me, you can't and don't want to be the only positive influencer in your new client's life. You won't be able to handle it, especially if you are doing your job well and your business is growing.

Let go of the fear of not being in complete control of them and allow them to find the people around them who will positively influence their lives. Even better, become the connector of positive influencers for your clients.

As your business grows so does your network of committed members. The best retention tool you have is connecting them to each other! You know by now what they struggle with and what they are committed to. Connect them to other people who have been through it and are now standing on the other side. Far too often trainers think that they must connect everyone to themselves. This is short sighted, and impossible to maintain. Your clients and potential members want to be a part of something bigger than themselves. Show them how they can be!

If you neglect the importance of the influencer, you have become The Faker, if you think you are the only one who can be the influencer, you have become The Taker. Be The Rainmaker and get ready for real results and real referrals!

Think Like A Rainmaker...

I know that like-minded people attract each other. I train my mind to respond quickly, and I am ready to make decisions quickly and confidently.

Put In The Work...

Go to a restaurant and do not open your menu until your waiter gets to the table, decide confidently what you will have to eat right on the spot.

You do not need to make all of your decisions in this way, but whenever possible train your mind to decide quickly.

What did this feel like? What did you order? Did you end up enjoying what you chose? How far did this take you out of your comfort zone?

_____

_____

_____

For The Bold...

Change the way you make decisions. Stop saying "I don't know," or "Let me think about it" in decision making situations and start saying "Yes" or "No" whenever possible. Take three days and keep a log of how many times you are faced with a decision and you wait to decide. Then look back over the list at the end of the three days and evaluate your decision making. Did you wait because it was wise and necessary? Or, were you unsure of yourself and didn't want to commit one way or the other? Let me hear about it: www.facebook.com/TrainingWithRyan

Chapter 11 - Step 6 Real Results & Real Referrals!

THE GOAL

If you have not already. Close the deal. Sign them up. Build referral sources.

THE WHY

It is time for them to officially commit to the opportunity that you are offering. If you're at the close and it doesn't happen here, you've missed something along the way.

THE SCENARIO

You are coming to the end of your conversation with a potential new client, Wanda Wantstobeaclient. She says:

- Thanks for all your help today! This place is great. I really hope that I can stick to a program this time, I'm famous for starting something and not really finishing it.

What do you do? What do you say? How would you respond?

Let's take a look at how Freddy Faker, Timmy Taker, and The Rainmaker respond.

THE RESPONSE

Freddy Faker

"It's been great talking to you. Like I said earlier, if you ever need anything at all just let me know."

-Thanks Freddy Faker, I appreciate your help. I hope I can get to my goals quickly. Like I said earlier, it has always been tough for me to stick with it, but I think this time will be different!

"Definitely, you'll do great, I'm excited for you. Keep working hard and it will all work out. Plus, I'll be around, and I'll check in on you from time to time."

- ...ok, thanks, talk to you later,...

What Happened Here???

On the surface it appears that Freddy Faker is being a genuinely nice guy. Not too pushy, not too salesy, just offering to help whenever it is needed. But here is the problem – the conversation is ending and he knows that Wanda needs help, she knows she needs help, but Freddy never asks to get her started! They both know that if she walks away and doesn't make a financial commitment to this, she is going back to her old ways and will never really hit her goals. But he lets her go. He'd rather be comfortable. He'd rather wait for someone who "really wants to train with me." He never plans to follow up with her, her friends, or anyone else for that matter. He just puts a blanket statement out there "if you ever need anything at all." This is an absolutely wonderful thing to say in the correct context, but when you know they are ready to buy, don't make them wait around any longer. Sign them up, close the deal and start building a solid referral base by having one more perfectly satisfied client.

Timmy Taker

"So I have a training contract here for 25 sessions. You'll need to buy these now and we can start tomorrow."

- I don't know if I can really afford 25 right now.

"Look, it's the best deal for you and plus, if you're not committed to this, then there isn't any point any way. I've got other people to meet with."

- No, I am committed, I just don't know…

"What's there not to know? You sign up, you start training, you hit your goals. Let's do this! You don't want to be back where you were three months ago do you?"

- No, that's not it. I just… feel like you aren't really listening to me. Something just doesn't feel right to me…

"Wanda, I understand. I bet you'd feel better if you had a friend to work out with. Who else do you know that would be ready to join you tomorrow for our session? Let's get a group together and make sure you have some more accountability too!"

- I'm sorry, I made a mistake. I'll have to give you a call another time…

What Happened Here???

By now Timmy Taker should make your skin crawl. The further into the sales process you get the more natural it should feel and that's not what happened here. Timmy Taker jumped straight to the close and he seems to immediately care more about referrals than about the person directly in front of him. The only way to get a recommendation or for someone to genuinely refer someone to you is to show them how great it is in the first place. Don't be Timmy Taker and jump the gun.

The Rainmaker

"Wanda, it's been really great talking with you, thanks for sharing everything you have so far."

- Thanks, I just know that I have to make a change.

"I know this is really important to you and you are really committed. Many of my clients started out exactly the way you are now. You aren't as far from your goal as you think you are."

- Do you really think so?

"Definitely, if we stick to this, three months from now you'll feel like a new person and in six months you'll be ready for that reunion you've been talking about. I am really excited for you."

- Yes, me too! My husband and daughter are really excited for me too.

"And, I know money was a concern at fir-"

- But, you know what, I know this is important and if I don't get this right in my life then everything else feels out of place.

"Are there any other questions I can answer for you before we get started and set up our next session?"

- Where do I sign?

"Right here. As we talked about earlier, we have our three month and six month goals set. We'll start with 3x a week in the gym with me for the first goal, but I will require that you do some homework on your own or with friends outside of here as well. At that point we will do a complete reevaluation and see what needs to be adjusted in your goals and your workouts. The first three months will total $2,520. Here you go."

- Thanks, that works perfect, we're all set. Is there anything else I need to know?

"All that I ask of everyone that I train is that you be completely honest with me in everything I ask you to do. And as we start doing this and you start seeing results, please take the time to tell someone about what you're doing."

- Ok, I can do that. You know I've been so excited, and my family is behind me 100%, I can't wait to tell my friend Donna Doeswhateverido!

"That's perfect, tell them, and tell Donna. I'm sure before long they will want to be getting the same results that you will be seeing! Plus, this will do two big things for you, 1. It will start to build your confidence that you are actually making a change and 2. It will help you stay accountable to your goal. When you tell someone what you are doing, then you really have to do it! Plus, this is how my business has grown so much, people like you working hard and wanting their friends and family to experience the same results too! Thank you so much for that in advance."

- I will definitely do that! We haven't even really worked out yet and I have already had a better time with you than anywhere else. I feel like you really care and have taken the time to listen.

"Thanks Wanda, that means a lot, In fact, is there anyone that you are thinking of now that you know can use my services?"

- Now that you mention it, my husband could really use this too and I know Donna would come if I asked her to.

"That's a great start. The people close to you are the ones that can impact you the most, and you can have an impact on their lives as well."

- You are absolutely right. This is perfect!

"I've got you on my calendar. Go talk to your husband and to Donna, and I will see you in two days! You're ready!"

- I can't wait!

What Happened Here???

How did the Rainmaker make this work? When the time came to close the deal, the Rainmaker had everything lined up and ready to go. This turns the toughest most awkward part of the sales process into the most simple, exciting, and easy part! The dreaded close becomes a launching point into the training sessions and into referring new clients and members. Once they know that you truly do care about them (1. Do they know that I care?), they will be willing to open up and share any pains or needs with you (2. Ouch, Where's the Pain?). From here it is very simple to find out how committed they are (3. Committed or just Complaining?), how much they value your service (4. Top Dollar?), and who else is helping them make their final decision (5. Outside Influences?). If at any point this doesn't feel right or it doesn't flow to the next step naturally, they have failed the current step and we need to bring it back.

THE CHALLENGE

It's been said that "you can't convince anyone to buy anything, you can just be there for them when they are ready to buy." I don't 100% disagree with this statement. It is true that we are not here to manipulate. BUT, at the same time we will not just be order takers, giving our services only to the people who ask for them. We must inspire change, help them to see a new vision of who they can become, and be there to serve and help them reach their goals!

Closing the deal should feel natural, not forced. If it doesn't feel like the next step in the progression then it is likely that something was missed along the way. Or that you need more practice getting there.

3 Natural Ways To Close The Sale…

1. **Silence** – Signing up should be the next natural progression if every other test is passed, chances are you might be talking yourself out of the sale when all they need to do is process the info and ask you one final question, let them.

2. **Set dates** – Be specific and immediate, look back to the time frames you learned about when getting to know their commitment level, finding out their pain and needs, and work toward them.

3. **Show them the way** – Give them your professional opinion. This can be very effective if you know you, like you and trust you (which they should at this point). Often we are too hesitant to just flat out tell them what we honestly believe they should do. Knowing their budget, time frame and goals all help you make this recommendation more specialized. But, don't be afraid if they can't afford it or don't agree with you, you are offering them what is best for them. Think back to our example of the doctor offering advice to you as his patient, it doesn't matter if you don't love the advice or agree with advice, your doctor is going to give you his best, unbiased, professional opinion. If he didn't because he was afraid of how you would feel then he would be a horrible doctor. As fitness professionals we should take a similar approach when 'prescribing' what is best for our clients in our professional scope. There is nothing wrong with saying: "In my professional opinion, your best option is..." But, you better know your stuff, and you'd better be honest, you cannot afford to get the reputation that so many Timmy Taker's in our industry have.

When Is The Best Time To Ask For A Referral?

As soon as the deal is done. As soon as they are satisfied with what they have. Remember, people feel good when they have made a decision to change. Allow them to share that feeling with others! You should be asking for the referral when they close or at the latest within their first two sessions. Freddy Faker in me rises up here and says "Isn't that too soon? I don't want to be pushy. They'll bring people if they like it and are getting results." Maybe they will and maybe they won't, not everyone thinks that way. If you have done every other step along the way and are willing to go through the careful process of following these steps with the potential client or member that they are referring, it won't feel pushy at all.

Think about the last time you bought something that you were excited about – a new phone, car, TV? You were so excited about it, you wanted to show it off, you wanted people to notice. Or what about that restaurant that you love, you can't help but tell your friends about it! It is natural to sell the things we love and are excited about to the people around us that we care about. Here is the difference – your clients don't have anything physical in their hands to show off to their friends when they sign up with you. And once they've hit their goals it's almost too late to start. A gradual consistent change is something that your clients will easily overlook.

It is your job to show them their results and encourage them. It is your job here to help your new client find the words to talk about what they are becoming more and more passionate about. It is you job to create the environment and expectation of the referral. You may not even want to call them referrals simply because it sounds too business/sales like. Whatever you call them, make them happen. And they will only happen with your direct attention to them. Without your guidance your clients and members are only talking about an idea, air, a goal. You are the one that makes it concrete, you are the one that makes it something that they can be a part of and that others want to be a part of too. Serve and inspire them so much that they inspire others.

Here are the three most important things to remember with referrals, as you follow each step in the I HATE Selling System:

1. Follow up with them.

2. Follow up with them.

3. Follow up with them.

Do these if you want to be Timmy Taker...

> Jump straight to the close

> Care more about referrals than the person in front of you

Do these if you want to be Freddy Faker...

>Never close

>Don't ask for referrals

Think Like A Rainmaker...

I know that people feel good when they have just made a decision to change. I want to teach them to have the confidence and ability to share that excitement with others!

Put In The Work...

List the six steps in the I HATE Selling Sales Process. Explain the goal and most important part of each step. Circle the one that you need the most help with and write out why.

1. _____
2. _____
3. _____
4. _____
5. _____
6. _____

I need the most help with this step and here is why...

_____

_____

_____

_____

_____

For The Bold...

Message me to set up a consultation take your business to the next level. I help people just like you everyday and I'd love to help you too! www.facebook.com/TrainingWithRyan

Part 3 - Go!

Chapter 12 - Twelve Top Rainmaker Tips

The Hardest Part...

This chapter could have gone on and on forever, so instead of telling you every little thing about every single person that has influenced me, I forced myself to cut it down to 12 quick thoughts and principles. For those of you on this list, you have had an impact in my life beyond what I have words for, thank you. Many of the men and women on this list I know personally and meet with weekly, many I have had the honor of working with, and some I have learned from by reading or watching from afar. My goal in sharing these is to inspire you to keep learning and for you to find others that will help you and push you to be the Rainmaker you were meant to become. The bottom line is this, I couldn't make it on my own, you can't make it on your own. We need to be constantly learning and growing and being held accountable. I need to be pushed to my limit and then some. I need someone to bounce my ideas off of and for someone to tell me to "Go for it!" or "Stop it." If you need that mentor that so many of us have found success with, my contact information is at the end of this chapter. Because this is what others have done for me, this is what I am now striving to do for others.

What I Have Learned From Rainmakers in Other Fields...

1. **It's All About Relationships** - Pastor Mark Evans, Senior Pastor, Northwest Orlando

   This seems so simple but it is so easy to overlook. When I get too busy, or too tired, or even too driven for that matter, this seems to be the first thing to go. But when I remember that people matter the most and relationships drive everything, I am able to help on a deeper level, do more than I thought possible, and stop from getting overwhelmed.

www.northwestorlando.com

2. **Momentum is the Second Most Powerful Force on the Planet** – Rick Strombeck, Head Honcho, Strombeck Consulting CPA

When things are going bad, it's as if nothing could ever go right. But when things are going right, it's like nothing could ever go wrong. If you've ever watched a basketball you know that it is a game of "runs." One team will hit their stride and go on a run and score 12 points while the other team will only score three or four in the same time frame. It rarely happens where both teams are scoring back and forth, one almost always has the momentum on their side and when they do, they can't be stopped. Learn how to use momentum to your advantage and it change the way you view business.

www.strombeck.com

3. **Do Not Despise Small Beginnings** – Pastor Sergio Hornung, Head Pastor, Agua Viva, Lima Peru

It can be so difficult to get started when you feel so small, but we must remember that it is good to see the work begin. I remember just starting out, not knowing how to sell, not knowing how to train or progress well at all. But it grew and it continues to grow. Everyone starts somewhere, what is your story going to be?

4. **Under-Promise, Over-Deliver** - Micah Mackubin, Controller, uBreak iFix

You don't have to have the most outgoing personality, you don't have to be a natural born salesman. You can simply follow the proper system, do excellent work, and honestly care for people and you will be successful. Do what you say you will do. The Faker under-delivers, the Taker over-promises, The Rainmaker under-promises and over-delivers and everyone he works withs loves it.

5. **Get A Mentor… Or Two… Or Three… Or…** - David Bouton, Charles Clayton Construction

   You cannot be successful in this life on your own. There are older men and women out there, more experienced experts in the field that you want to be in and in the areas of business that you want to be excellent in, and they are looking for someone to pour their knowledge into. Learn to ask the right questions and don't be afraid to put yourself out there and you will find people willing to help you along the way.

6. **Proper Process Protects against Pressure** – Peter Brunton, COO, Vigorous Design

   When I realized how stressed out I was feeling because of my disorganization, I knew things needed to change. I began setting processes for all of my training sessions, evaluations, and screenings. I set aside time to purposely organize and reevaluate my processes. This little saying changed so much for me and still does to this day.

7. **Start with Why** - Simon Sinek, Speaker, Writer

   If you haven't read Simon Sinek's famous book, "Start with Why" you are missing out. Everyone knows WHAT they do, some know HOW they do it, but very few can go deep enough to understand and explain WHY. Start with his TED Talk and then go out and get the book.

8. **Don't Be Afraid to Work and Work Hard** - Mike Rowe, Founder, Mike Rowe Works

   If you haven't seen Mike Rowe on any of his shows, you are doing yourself a disservice. There has been a saying that has gained a lot of traction lately. It started innocently enough, but has since strangely morphed into something else altogether, as things often do. The thought is, "work smarter, not harder." But, this thought assumes that the worker is already working as hard as he or she can in the first place. When we simply say that we want to work smarter and not harder, we start to make excuses to not work hard in the first place.

9. **Live Like No One Else So That Later You Can Live Like No One Else** - Dave Ramsey, Founder, Ramsey Solutions

If you aren't in control of your finances it is almost impossible to dream, grow or build your business the way you want to. No matter how hard you work, if you are filling in a bucket that has a whole in it, you can't see real success and it will drain you. Take control of your finances, take control of your business, take control of your life. "Live like no one else, so that later you can live like no one else." - Dave Ramsey

10. **Inspiring Is Better Than Teaching** - Grace McKenzie, The Lovely Project

When someone is inspired they become self-motivated, they will go and learn, they will go and practice, they will ask for help. My beautiful wife always seems to have the right perspective in any tough situation. Teaching does very little but inspiring impacts lives. When we look to only teach we can very quickly become judgmental. When we look to inspire we are able to get into others situations and show empathy. Having mercy on yourself, and having mercy on others, can be the start of real inspiration. My wife lives this every day and it reminds me of the one true maker of the rain, our Father in Heaven.

www.thelovelyproject.org

www.wearelovely.com

11. **Think Good Thoughts** - Karen McKenzie, KRM Consulting

Growing up my mom would always tell us to "think good thoughts." She replies to every email with "think good thoughts." And as a kid, I hated it... mainly because I didn't understand it. Just like so many of these other Rainmaking thoughts and ideas, it seems so simple. But it's simplicity makes it practical and possible to apply. The more good thoughts that you have running through your mind, the more positive ideas, attitude, and energy you have at your disposal. So, Think Good Thoughts. Rainmakers do.

12. **I've Got an Idea... and, if You Love What You Do, You'll Never Have a Job** - Jim McKenzie, Hi-Tech Video (My Dad)

"I've got an idea." My dad was never short on ideas, I loved that about him and I inherited that from him. Don't let the people around you who are afraid to step out and do the impossible tell you that what you are doing is impossible. Go, dream, do. Who knows what could happen? I know what will happen if you don't, nothing.

"If you love what you do, you'll never have a job." This was written in permanent marker on a white board in my dad's office for as long as I can remember and it stuck with me too. My dad loved football, he played football, he coached football, he watched football, he talked football. One day one of his "ideas" was to start a recruiting service to help kids in the area be seen better by college scouts. This idea turned into his dream job. Every school in the country that recruited kids out of Florida sent their recruiting coordinators, assistant coaches, and even head coaches to our house to watch tape, drink beer, and talk football. The list of top coaches that I have sat down to dinner with or watched silently as they looked over tape and talked about kids they were thinking of recruiting with my dad amazes me. My dad found that rare combination of something he loved, something he was good at, and something no one else was doing. His "office" was a garage turned man-cave with 10-11 televisions with satellite hookups on each, VCRs, and VHS tapes lining every wall (yes it was a while ago, VHS, VCR & satellite TV...) with every high school football team in the state on tape ready to watch at their fingertips. It was fun and when you can make work fun you are often able to work even harder at it.

This is by no means a complete list of all the people who have poured their valuable time and experience into my life. The point is, you need people around you who are better than you, who are more experienced than you, who you will disagree with, who will challenge you. Go out and make that a part of your life, it will change you. Follow these steps in the I HATE Selling sales process and your business will grow, and you will start to HATE horrible sales and service as much as I do. Keeping working, keep practicing, keep seeking advice, that is what it takes to silence Freddy Faker and Timmy Taker and become The Rainmaker.

For The Bold...

If you are ready to get serious about growing your business, I am available for personal coaching and business development. I am always looking for good people to work with who want to grow and who want to help others achieve their goals!

I am here for you too. Those who have grown the most and have taken their business to the next level make the commitment to themselves and those they are working with, will you?

www.facebook.com/TrainingWithRyan

Made in the USA
Middletown, DE
26 July 2018